HOW TO STOP GIVING YOURSELF AWAY

RACHEL STONE

Copyright © 2022 by Rachel Stone

All rights reserved.

No part of this book may be reproduced in any form or by any electronic or mechanical means, including information storage and retrieval systems, without written permission from the author, except for the use of brief quotations in a book review.

Claim Your Freebie NOW!

Get Good At Problem Solving

Want to know the secret behind getting good at problem solving? Everyone seems to be able to do it, but you're stuck in the pile of endless to-do lists with little progress.

Ok, so how do I get my FREE book?

EASY! See the next page

Claim Your Freebie NOW

Instructions:

1. Open the camera or the QR reader application on your smartphone.
2. Point your camera at the QR code to scan the QR code.
3. A notification will pop-up on screen.
4. Click on the notification to open the website link

Contents

Introduction	ix
1. Establishing a foundation	1
2. PEOPLE-PLEASING	5
The draining effects of people-pleasing	6
Reasons why pleasing others is detrimental	7
How pleasing others may exhaust those who appreciate us	7
People-pleasing's profound origins	8
3. SELF-GASLIGHTING	14
What is Gaslighting?	14
Signs that make you doubt yourself	18
How gaslighting affects people	20
How to survive a gaslighter	23
4. SEEKING VALIDATION FROM OTHERS	27
Validation from others	28
Abusing 'shoulds'	28
No matter how hard you try, the world will not bend to your will	31
The importance of correct reasoning	33
5. NOT BEING NICE IS ALRIGHT	38
Being "nice"	42
It's good not to be kind	48
6. STAYING IN TOXIC RELATIONSHIPS WITH FRIENDS, PARTNERS AND PARENTS	52
How to stop worrying about what other people think and remain calm	53
Take action to end the use of manipulation methods	57
Managing obtrusive people	59
The best ways to make and keep friends and have a meaningful social life	61
Love at any cost	69

7. Reaching your big goals and stop people-pleasing   74
8. SET HEALTHY BOUNDARIES WITHOUT FEAR   83
   Defining a boundary   83
   Setting healthy boundaries in your relationships with friends   85
   Family relationships: How to set healthy boundaries   87
   Workplace boundaries: How to set them right   89

Conclusion   91
Feedback   93

Introduction

The dilemma with pleasing people is that you're well aware of how it's happening yet unable to stop it. In addition, whatever the other person suggests won't make you happy. To-do lists, commitments to friends, financial commitments, or an intangible sense of pressure to excel in everything you do all at once may be making you feel overburdened. A lack of time to accomplish what you truly care about, such as spending quality time with your loved ones or being alone without feeling guilty, might leave you feeling irritated. With so many demands on our time, it's too easy to get tossed about and lose sight of what's important.

Sometimes it seems that pleasing others is a harmless endeavour. We end ourselves doing things we don't want to because we can't say no, and we soon forget what we like doing.

As a peacekeeper, it's always hard and difficult to keep everyone pleased. Every circumstance necessitates a particular approach and set of abilities. You may have to be a sympathetic ear to a friend's woes, or you may have to be the one who has to go shopping or to a certain restaurant even if you don't want to. You may have to be both. As time passes, you grow more disconnected from your actual self until you eventually lose yourself completely.

Even when you believe you'll love something, the fear of saying no keeps you from participating. Ideally, you'd prefer to attend the family reunion. Still, what if you find yourself in an uncomfortable circumstance and are unable to say no? Slowly, you begin to prefer a life of isolation because it is more secure.

Everything in your life is affected by people-pleasing, from the workplace and family to friends and colleagues. When you're in the midst of it, you lose your motivation and energy, and you cannot reach your goals.

Where are you right now?

Do you feel like you are constantly putting your needs last and paying the price?

Why did I write this book?

Because there is a need for it, I polled my audience, and these were the results:

Do you put others' needs before your own regularly?
78% said YES
22% said NO

Have you said 'Yes' far too many times for fear of upsetting people?
77% said YES
23% said NO

Have you stayed in an unhealthy relationship/friendship for too long for fear of upsetting the other person?
77% said YES
23% said NO

The fact that you've got a front-row ticket to life's events doesn't mean you have to be anxious about it.

While this twenty-first-century chaos is a reality, there is an option that allows you to regulate your own life and not allow others to have excessive influence or control over you. There is a tangible method available for enhancing your well-being on all levels (at work, home, and play), developing self-respect, and fostering a more positive self-image.

The answer to all of this is simple: **set boundaries.** Real change may happen in any aspect of your life, provided you have the right principle in place.

What defines a boundary? When it comes to our behaviour and how we connect with others, these are the options we make. A kind of personal code that is subject to alteration depending on the situation. Boundaries will be explained in more detail in the future section, but for now, keep in mind that a boundary is quite simply where you draw the line.

What's the big deal? Because life on this planet has changed so dramatically in the last 30 years, we can't simply follow the same behaviour patterns that worked for prior generations. We now live in a civilisation that is always switched on and always linked to the rest of the world, even if we don't realise it.

Few of us have developed plans to deal with new issues in our fast-paced world. With social media, high-speed and high-turnover lovers, increasing workloads in the face of new technologies, and a culture of perfectionism in parenting and relationships, these are just some of the challenges that modern families confront. Many of us still face old issues, such as the consequences of divorce, personality disputes, the anxieties of being trapped in the age gap, and professional concerns.

Let me show you how it's possible to keep up with your desire to serve others—it's a fantastic trait to have. As well as teaching you how to keep this under control, I'll also show you how to prioritise your well-being above that of others. The purpose of this book is to accomplish just that. We'll work together to devise a strategy for shifting your perspective from one of emptiness to one of self-awareness and delight in life's journey.

People-pleasing is broken down into phases that follow a logical progression. We'll learn how to be assertive and not worry about what other people think of our thoughts and emotions and how to control our anxiety about other people's responses. You'll become a master of your social circumstances, relationships, and profession.

We'll go through various methods and resources to assist you in getting started on the path to a more fulfilling existence. As a starting point, it's important to grasp precisely what "people-pleasing" is and how it's ingrained in your personality. If you're ready to start saying no, and stop giving yourself away, then let's take the first step forward together.

1

Establishing a foundation

A FRIEND once requested if she might stay with me for a few days a few years back. We had a month-long stay together, during which time I answered yes to everything she asked. During this period, she didn't pay rent, didn't assist around the home, enlisted my help in her time-consuming and stressful decision-making processes, and was visibly startled when I asked her to purchase toilet paper only once. I found her presence in my home very stressful, but I felt it would be wrong of me to ask her to go or expect more from her than she appeared ready to provide. I put my well-being on hold in favour of hers because I cared more about how she felt. We're no longer friends, by the way.

After a few years, I had to return to my parents' home, which was several hours away from most of my friends. I regularly met with a group of these friends to play board games, but I couldn't participate unless someone was willing to let me stay the night afterwards. I was able to sleep on a friend's couch for a short time. Even though I think I'm a much better house guest than my friend who recently stayed with me, the fact remains that I was someone who was regularly in someone else's space for longer than he wanted me to be there, which can be a stressful experience. After a while, my friend informed me that he could no longer accommodate me. In other words, he put his desires ahead of my own. We've been friends for a long time, and we're still in touch.

Many of us believe that nothing is more essential than giving our time, money, and energy away to others, and I am no exception. We may have a boss who wants us to work on a big project until it is completed, only for that boss to get all the credit. Alternatively, we may have a close friend who often contacts us to vent about her woes or beg for favours that primarily benefit her. Or maybe our mother wants us to be a part of her new fitness regime for the rest of her life. It doesn't matter what the circumstances are; we give all we have to these folks without hesitation and rarely get anything.

Giving yourself away can mean doing the following:

- People-pleasing.
- Gaslighting yourself.
- Seeking validation from others.
- Staying in toxic relationships/friendships.
- Living for other people/taking care of them first.
- Giving up on your goals due to others.

All of this is connected in some manner. In general, though, it comes down to disregarding your own needs.

Gifting isn't always a terrible thing, though. Helping others is a noble and kind deed that most of us have experienced and benefited from when we've been in a position to need it. Even the good ones have a limit. When we give away all of our time, money, and energy to others, we leave ourselves with nothing.

Women, especially, are taught that their own needs are secondary to those of others, so it may not be that surprising that many of us give ourselves away. However, as much as we may value others, the one on whom we rely the most is ourselves. When it comes to our well-being, we are individually the most important person in our own life, and we need to treat ourselves as we treat others, if not more.

Learning to love and care for ourselves is a major theme in this book. Giving to oneself is all about self-love and self-care in its simplest form. However, there is more to it than that. It comes down to respecting our genius and putting out the effort to improve that brilliance to become smarter, fitter, more creative, or any other way that we choose to be. We're not only taking care of ourselves; we're also investing in ourselves by doing this.

We can't invest in ourselves if we always give it to others. Taking care of oneself first may appear selfish if we're raised to think that we should constantly put others before ourselves. However, investment in ourselves is not just important for personal satisfaction and self-esteem. When we take care of our own needs first, we can better help others around us. It's similar to having a savings account. We'll run out of money if we keep taking money out of this account without adding anything. If, on the other hand, we put the account's well-being first, it would fill up faster and have more money in it, allowing us to make more withdrawals. First and foremost, we must take care of ourselves. Then, we will be better able to help others.

Investing in one's well-being will look different for everyone, but here are a few suggestions to get you started:

Learn to say no

A previous buddy took full advantage of my uncompromising hospitality. This put me under a lot of pressure and ruined a good relationship. Perhaps our relationship might have survived if I had been able to say "no" to her when I reached my limit, as my buddy could say to me. A difficult task for someone who tends to give, saying "no" is sometimes required. If the person you say "no" to respects you, however, there will be no bitter feelings.

Let go of unnecessarily difficult relationships: Certain individuals in our lives need a lot of our time and attention, but the rewards they provide us much outweigh the costs. On the other hand, some individuals may not give as generously as they get. If you know somebody like this, it's a good idea to evaluate whether or not they're worth preserving in your life. Consider letting these folks go if the effort is not worthwhile.

Take care of your health

We've all heard how important it is to take care of our bodies, but I'm bringing it up again since its significance cannot be overstated. To be of any use to ourselves or others, we need to be in peak physical and mental health. One of the finest investments you can make in yourself is to fulfil those objectives no matter your health priorities.

Set goals

Investing in ourselves is more than simply making sure we're in decent health. According to a recent BitQT in Test poll, dedicating time to self-improvement is also important. Consider the goals you have for the foreseeable future. Maybe you aspire to be able to sprint a mile unabated. You may want to master new skills, such as driving, coding, or even cooking. Make a list of the skills and knowledge you'd want to gain and work toward reaching those objectives.

Giving to others may be a selfless and compassionate act. On the other hand, if we are always giving to others, we may run out of resources to devote to ourselves. We're indeed the most important person in our life, and as such, we must invest in ourselves. Investing in ourselves improves our self-esteem and ability to give to others, but it also helps us better love and cherishes ourselves.

2

People-Pleasing

A PEOPLE-PLEASER IS TOO CONCERNED with what others think of them. They lack self-confidence and are always looking for other people's approval. The degree to which one tries to please as many people as possible varies tremendously. For example, a certain group of individuals, such as coworkers or bosses, might be the source of the problem.

Even though children are considered a great delight to their teachers, they are often unable to follow through on any requests from their parents. At the same time, it shows that the desire to provide joy to others isn't only a child's trait; it may persist into adulthood. It is common for teenagers to struggle with the conflict between wanting to fit in with their peers and wanting to be an individual.

For individuals with a people-pleasing condition, the issue engulfs them from early morning till late night. They are afraid of causing a disturbance by expressing their views. Even if they are questioned, they will provide responses that others want to hear rather than their own. Concerns about how others see them will keep them up at night.

There is also the fear of saying no, which results in a hasty 'yes' answer. When the thought of saying no makes you sick to your stomach, your life has been taken away from you. Because of the guilt of saying no in the past, many people avoid saying no in the future because they don't want to offend anybody again.

Picking out clothing for the day is a basic illustration of this. People-pleasers are unlikely to dress in a way that gives them confidence and relaxation. Instead, they'll wear something that other people will like, which is more acceptable. Even the purchase of clothing will be made based on what other people think of the clothing, rather than what the wearer thinks of the clothing themselves.

People-pleasing is difficult to identify as a problem since we are taught that being polite and considering other people's feelings is vital. A desire to be accepted and please others is good quality, but when you bend over yourself to the point that it affects your well-being, you have a problem.

The draining effects of people-pleasing

Life is a constant source of exhaustion for the people-pleaser. Everything from eating Chinese food when you wanted Italian to changing cities because your lover requested it may rob you of a sliver of your happiness.

Your whole existence is committed to making the lives of others better. In your heart, you want to assist them and find a solution. In other cases, individuals are naive enough to believe that this isn't a big deal. Every act you do on behalf of someone consumes some of your own time and resources. Another thing to keep in mind is that this isn't always negative.

The problem is that when you put all of your energy into making others happy, you end up feeling worn out. Particularly when the people in your life keep coming back with new difficulties for you to deal with and more concerns that you don't want to be engaged in.

If you always strive to assist others, you will become exhausted and depleted. It's tough to make an imperfect world perfect. When you put the needs of others ahead of your own, you may end up feeling overwhelmed and alone, as if you have too many obligations and no one to help you.

Those with a people-pleasing condition can't cease doing what they're doing simply. Your desire to make people happy is likely to continue despite being exhausted and irritated. This is the point at which the issue becomes dangerous.

Reasons why pleasing others is detrimental

In certain cases, the condition might make you feel smothered and develop further medical problems. I became depressed because of the pressure to please, saying yes to everything, and focusing on other people's emotions instead of my own.

According to research published in the journal Natural Neuroscience, people-pleasing might modify your behaviour and reduce your feeling of integrity. To get the response you want in a discussion, you begin to make little white falsehoods. Initially, these little white lies aren't dangerous, but they make it easier to tell larger, more destructive lies over time. Before you realise it, you've transformed into someone at odds with yourself and are entangled in a web of deception.

In addition, people-pleasing is an indication of inadequacy in self-awareness. We're so anxious to please others that we'll frequently say yes to things we don't want to do just to avoid looking terrible in their eyes. We put ourselves in harm's way when we overindulge in alcohol, engage in illicit drug use, or speed while driving.

How pleasing others may exhaust those who appreciate us

People-pleasing might be challenging even for those who care about us and can tell that we're having difficulty dealing with our issues. It's heartbreaking to see someone go through pain because they can't prioritise their own needs. It might be hard to try to make someone else happy while also acknowledging their inability to articulate their true emotions. It takes a lot of time and effort, and it may even drive people apart from each other.

There's no need to feel any worse about yourself than you already do. When you learn to say no, you can look forward to your loved ones being a bit more relieved that life is going the way you want it.

People-pleasing's profound origins

People-pleasers suffer from the condition to please because their warped thinking is trapped in a cycle of self-defeating behaviour. In this group, your people-pleasing is motivated by a firm belief that you need and should seek the approval of all of your acquaintances. Doing what's best for others is the only way to assess your self-worth and establish your identity.

If you have a people-pleasing mindset, behaving politely is thought to protect you from being rejected or subjected to other unpleasant treatment from others. Despite this, you desire widespread approval while imposing strict standards and severe judgment on yourself. In other words, you've thought your way into the situation, and you'll have to think your way out of it to get yourself back on track. That is why you must begin by examining and fixing your people-pleasing mindset.

People-pleaser habits

People-pleasers are compelled to put the needs of others ahead of their own, a condition known as the **'desire to please.'** Those who fall into this category tend to do too much for others, never say "no," seldom delegate, and become overcommitted and overextended. Your desire for others' acceptance drives you to engage in self-defeating, stressful behaviours, which may hurt your health and the health of your closest relationships. Understanding and breaking your self-defeating people-pleasing tendencies is the greatest first step if you fall into this category.

'Desire to please' is largely an avoidance strategy designed to keep you safe from the unpleasant feelings of resentment, disagreement, and confrontation that you associate with it. However, as you may have guessed, the strategy is flawed. As long as you avoid situations, your worries will only grow.

You never learn how to handle conflict efficiently or cope with anger because you avoid challenging emotions correctly. Consequently, you give up too much power to those who would rule over you by fear and deception.

The quickest way to focus and begin your development process is to identify your dominant side.

Being a people-pleaser has hidden costs

Making others happy is a strange task. Initially, it may not appear like an issue at all. 'People-pleaser' is a label you could proudly wear as praise or a nice description of yourself.

What's wrong with attempting to make other people happy, after all? If we care about the individuals we care about, shouldn't we all do our best to improve their lives? More people-pleasers, surely, would make the world a better place, wouldn't they?

People-pleasing is a cute moniker for many people's major psychiatric issues.

Compulsive, even addictive, behaviour is the hallmark of the 'desire to please'. The drive to please others and an addiction to their approval rule you as a people-pleaser. At the same time, you have a sense of helplessness in the face of the burdens and demands these requirements have placed on your life.

Even if you've been diagnosed with the condition, your desire to please people goes well beyond just answering "yes" to their requests, invitations or demands. For those of us who are more concerned with pleasing others than ourselves, our emotional tuning knobs are stuck on a certain frequency. Your people-pleasing reaction mechanism kicks into high gear when you get the slightest inkling that someone else could need your assistance.

With so much focus on the needs of others, you frequently ignore the inner voice that tells you that overextending yourself or acting against your self-interests might be detrimental to your well-being.

Self-worth is entwined with how much you do for others and

how well you succeed if you suffer from the sickness to please. The secret to acquiring affection and self-worth and protecting yourself from desertion and rejection is to fulfil the needs of others. However, in practice, this is an utterly ineffective formula.

People-pleasers will go to great lengths to please others, even if it means sacrificing their well-being. However, the need to gain others' favour might make it difficult to take action. The fear of being rejected (the other side of the desire for approval) might paralyse you if you attempt to please many people at once, leaving you torn between right and wrong. What's the best option? What if you fail to please anyone?

How much does it cost to be nice?

People-pleasers have a hard time letting go of the belief that they are kind people and that they are seen as such by others. Their basic identity is based on this picture of friendliness. In reality, people's price for being kind is still much too high, even if they assume that being polite would keep them safe from bad circumstances with friends and family.

Firstly, since you are so kind, others may use and manipulate you. Because you're so pleasant, you can be oblivious to how you're being taken advantage of. Furthermore, putting on a happy face always inhibits you from expressing your true feelings, even if you have good reason to be angry.

As a second step, you refrain from criticising others so that you won't be criticised. To avoid confrontation, psychologists refer to this strategy as conflict avoidance. If you'd rather avoid criticism than conflict or anger, then avoid them at all costs.

Afraid of what others may think of you?

You're overly kind because you're afraid of feeling bad about yourself.

Fears of rejection, abandonment, conflict or confrontation, criticism, being alone, and rage all play a role in people-pleasing behaviour. As a people-pleaser, you believe that you will prevent unpleasant feelings in yourself and others if you are constantly kind and helpful to others. This idea has a two-way effect: it makes people more protective. First, you use your niceness to prevent and avoid negative feelings targeted at you from others—as long as you're so pleasant and constantly strive to do things to please people, why would anybody want to be upset, or reject or condemn you? For one thing, your self-centredness prevents you from feeling or expressing unfavourable feelings toward others.

To avoid nagging doubts, uncertainties, and persistent concerns, it is best to focus on being authentic rather than being pleasant.

Becoming accepted and accepted by others will always seem to be just out of grasp to the individual. There are no guarantees that your anxieties of being rejected or abandoned or confronted by an angry person will be lessened even if you succeed in satisfying others. As time goes on, they become ever more powerful.

People with the eagerness to please put up a mental barrier that prevents them from feeling or expressing these unpleasant feelings. Because of this, it damages the connections you work so hard to maintain and safeguard. Relationships lose their genuineness if you can't communicate your bad sentiments. One-dimensional cardboard representations are all that others will see of you, rather than the rich, multifaceted personality you are.

There is little hope of repairing a relationship if you're too kind to tell people what is making you sad, furious, disturbed, or disappointed—or if you're too nice to hear their concerns. When it comes to relationships, conflict avoidance isn't a necessary factor. Rather, it's a sign of a broken system. It's best to accept that conflicting emotions will inevitably arise and prepare yourself to cope.

Humans are hardwired to experience negative emotions. When someone tries to harm us or someone we care about, we are naturally built to experience fear and anger and react defensively. Conflict and anger may be effective communication tools if they are managed productively and conveyed correctly in the real world. If you handle them properly, these feelings may help you keep your relationships in excellent functioning order, with issues minimised and joys maximised.

Negative sentiments are a dangerous thing to ignore. When we try to hide our feelings of anger and resentment against another person, yet we are filled with anxiety, fear, and depression on the inside, how many of us have been there?

Migraines, tension headaches, back pain, nausea, elevated blood pressure, and a slew of other stress-related symptoms may all be signs of unpleasant repressed sentiments. A simmering hatred and dissatisfaction lurk under the surface, ready to burst into open hostility and rage. Your health and your closest relationships will suffer as a result of these physical and emotional issues in the long run.

You're not the only one going through this. One of the most common and debilitating illnesses in modern society is the 'desire to please,' which affects millions of people in the same way you do. Debilitating stress and tiredness might result from a constant need to please others at the price of your well-being. Alcohol, drugs, and/or food may be self-medication for people-pleasers who want to keep doing more for others despite exhaustion. Chronic fatigue syndrome, alcohol and drug misuse, eating disorders, and weight issues are linked to the 'desire to please.'

Even if you're a seasoned people-pleaser, you'll never be satisfied with your work, no matter how hard you try. Those you're trying to help whose needs you're trying to satisfy grow in number as time goes on. Trying extra harder to satisfy others will only exacerbate your feelings of shame and inadequacy due to the stress this causes and the consequent drain on your energy.

The metaphorical brick wall will be reached if you don't do anything to break the vicious cycle of pleasing others at the price of your happiness. You'll be fatigued and may even consider quitting.

You don't have to wait until you're at the point of no return to take action. You don't want your suppressed feelings of disappointment, rejection, and resentment to erupt into open hostility. A paralysing sadness might result from a repressed fury that never leaves your side.

If you allow the 'desire to please' pattern to run its course, you may develop emotions of shame, inadequacy, and failure. In the long run, long-suppressed resentment and anger become corrosive and may even lead to the breakup of beloved relationships. The ultimate fear of a people-pleaser, desertion, may become a horrific reality in the end.

People-pleasing is not a benign issue when seen in this way. Think of yourself as more than simply a good person who goes beyond in their efforts to make others happy or do too much for those you aim to please if you have the 'desire to please.'

But how can something that, on the surface, seems to be harmless and even beneficent end up being so destructive and problematic? Is it possible to explain how and why people-pleasing becomes a sickness?

Several self-defeating attitudes and faulty beliefs about yourself and others contribute to compulsive behaviour, which in turn is fuelled by a desire to avoid bad emotions that you've learned about as part of this course. People-pleasing syndrome, sometimes known as the 'desire to please' is characterised by faulty thinking, obsessive activity, and a desire to avoid unpleasant emotions.

The good news is that you have the power to prevent the spread of the condition and make a positive shift right now. Begin by making a tiny adjustment in one area of your life—your behaviour, beliefs, or feelings—and build from there. Like a stack of dominoes, your people-pleasing behaviours will eventually tumble over in defeat when you make one adjustment at a time.

What if you made more alterations to how you see yourself, think about yourself and act? Certainly. This will create a big change in your life. However, you should begin by taking tiny steps at a speed that works for you.

3

Self-Gaslighting

HOWEVER, while gaslighting is most usually connected with other people's abuse, it is possible to gaslight yourself as well.

Suppressing and denying your thoughts and feelings is prevalent in self-gaslighting. For example, after being harmed, you tend to assume, "I am probably exaggerating," or "Maybe it wasn't that awful."

"I didn't go through 'real' trauma."

"I wouldn't feel this way if I were a stronger or more spiritual person."

"He didn't truly mean what I assumed he meant."

"She didn't believe me because I'm not worth believing."

"I should be over it by now, rather than letting it affect every aspect of my life."

The reason you may be self-gaslighting is that you have been the victim of someone else's self-gaslighting in the past.

What is Gaslighting?

In abusive relationships, gaslighting is a common kind of manipulation. When an abuser or bully makes the victim doubt their reality and judgements, they engage in emotional abuse. Gaslighting victims begin to believe that they are gradually losing their sanity as a consequence. For the most part, gaslighting occurs in relationships between partners. But it is equally usual to find it in households or in dominating friendships. To wield power over others, toxic persons resort to such forms of emotional abuse. They are often motivated by a desire to manipulate family members, acquaintances, and even coworkers.

What is the process of gaslighting?

The tactic of "gaslighting" can distort one's view of the truth about a person. Gaslighting someone may cause you to doubt your memories, yourself, and your senses. The most probable outcome is that you'll be confused and wonder aloud whether there's anything wrong with you. In addition to making you doubt your sanity and judgment, it may leave you feeling unsure of yourself. There are times when it may be beneficial to know how a person who often gaslights others goes about their job.

What to keep an eye out for

You can tell whether someone is attempting to deceive you by looking for certain telltale signs. As a reminder, we'll have a look at some examples.

Disguise yourself for your own good

Anyone who is subjected to gaslighting is a serial and pathological liar. Even if it's there in front of your face, they won't budge or back down from their deception. It doesn't change anything, even if you present evidence of their lie or call them out. "Stop making stuff up" is the most prevalent thing they say. As a result, it may be claimed that lying is at the heart of the gaslighter's damaging activity. Even if you know they are lying, such individuals may be quite persuasive when you least expect it. As a consequence, you'll begin to doubt your judgment.

Discrediting you

You may be sure that individuals who gaslight you will be the ones who propagate untruths about you to others. They may seem to be concerned about you while at the same time telling others that you're insane or unstable mentally. Consider the possibility that such an approach may be quite successful. Some individuals don't even know the whole story when it comes to bullying and abuse. You may also be lied to by the bully, who may convince you that others feel the same way about you. These are the kind of folks who won't ever say anything negative about you. However, they will never miss an opportunity to persuade you to believe what they say about you to others.

Distract you

There is a good probability that a gaslighter will shift the conversation away from the issue at hand by asking follow-up questions instead of providing an answer. It will disrupt our thinking, but it will also make you rethink the need to press a subject when the bully does not feel like replying or reacting.

Reduce your emotions and ideas

The gaslighter will be able to manipulate you if you trivialise all of your feelings. They'll probably say things like, "You're being unduly sensitive," "Calm down," or "You're overreacting." As a result, you may believe that you are mistaken about your feelings or thoughts. A person who doesn't recognise your emotions, opinions, or views might cause you to doubt your own identity. There's more; you may never feel accepted or validated, which may be difficult to cope with at times.

Shift the blame

Gaslighting often employs the method of shifting responsibility. Regardless of how you attempt to conduct a conversation, you'll always be blamed for whatever happened. Even when you try to bring up how the abuser's conduct affects your feelings, gaslighters can derail the topic. They may get you to think that you are the root of the problem. Also, they may imply that if only you had acted differently, they wouldn't have treated you the way they do.

Refuse to accept any responsibility for your actions

When it comes to blaming others for their actions, abusers and bullies are masters of denial. They purposefully do this to avoid accepting responsibility for their terrible decisions. Denial like this may leave the victim feeling ignored, unnoticed, and as if their suffering has no bearing on the abuser. Such a strategy might make it difficult for a victim of abuse or bullying to recover and move on.

Use loving words as weapons

When confronted, a gaslighter will often respond with words of love and kindness. As a way to smooth things up, they do so. This person may say something like, "You're aware of how much I care about you?" Or, "I will never intentionally harm you." These words may be exactly what you're looking for. However, they cannot be considered legitimate, especially if the act is done repeatedly. As a result, people like this may be able to persuade you to let them off the hook, which is their main purpose.

Invent a new history

People who engage in gaslighting are more prone to recount the same tales repeatedly in ways that seem to be favourable to them. Even if your loved one pushes you to the ground, they may attempt to change the tale and pretend that you tripped over when you try to talk about it later. You crashed against the wall because they were attempting to steady you. Consequently, you may begin to distrust your memory of what occurred. All they want to achieve is a sense of uncertainty or doubt on your behalf.

There are several ways to use gaslighting, including minimising, distancing, blaming, and denying. Do not be distracted by their statements while dealing with someone who uses gaslighting as a manipulative tactic.

Signs that make you doubt yourself

Being a victim of gaslighting may lead to various psychological problems, such as suicide ideation and drug or alcohol addiction. Because of this, it's important to recognise when you're being gaslighted. If you think any of the following statements apply to you, you'll need to look at yourself.

- When you dispute your reality and emotions, it is hard for you to think that the treatment you are receiving is not awful or that you are being too sensitive to the experience.

- You don't believe what you're seeing or hearing. For whatever reason, you're afraid to express yourself. As you've learned, it's always better to keep your thoughts to yourself than to share them. As a result, you decide to keep your mouth shut.

- People around you make you feel vulnerable and uneasy like you're "stepping on eggshells." In addition, you have low self-esteem and a general sense of unease.

- The remarks of a gaslighter might cause you to believe that you are dumb, incorrect, mad, or inadequate. You may find yourself repeating the sentences repeatedly in your head.

- People around you think you're insane, unusual, or unstable like a gaslighter thinks you are. You feel helpless and alone. A situation like this might leave you feeling alone and confined.

- You are dissatisfied with who you have become: for example, you begin to believe that you are passive, weak, and used to be more forceful and powerful.

- Confusion is a possibility: The actions of a gaslighter may leave you perplexed. You may run across many representations of the same individual and get perplexed as to which one is the actual deal.

- Every day, you feel the need to apologise for everything you've done or the person you are.

- You believe you are too sensitive: The perpetrator rationalises unpleasant words or actions by claiming, "You need thicker skin" or "I was joking with you."

- When you spend time with a gaslighter, you get the impression that something terrible is about to happen. Unaware of the true cause, you may experience anxiety and/or fear.

- You're unsure about your judgment: Now and again, you start to question whether you recall everything that happened before. Sharing what you know may sometimes be discouraged due to the concern that it is incorrect.

- You're embarrassed by your perceived inadequacy: As a result, you may feel as if you're never going to measure up. Even if other people's needs and expectations are outlandish, you still give it your utmost to meet them.

- In your mind, you're always wondering what's wrong with you: You're always questioning whether or not there's anything wrong with you. In other words, you're worried that something is wrong with your mental state.

- You believe that other people are upset with you because of what you've done: You're always apologising for who you are and what you do. It's exhausting. You think that you are constantly untrustworthy or always making mistakes.

- Making judgments is tough for you since you don't trust yourself: You may tend to delegate crucial choices to acquaintances, family members, or your spouse. To avoid making any judgments at all, you are doing this.

How gaslighting affects people

As a consequence of its bizarre effects, gaslighting may lead to exploitation, which is difficult to perceive at times. A gaslighter's major goal is to undermine the victim's self-esteem and ability to make autonomous decisions in a planned and sophisticated manner. Consequently, the victim becomes a robot that follows the manipulator's directions. Gaslighting can do significant harm to the victim's emotional well-being. Gaslighting may lead to a person losing their self-identity if exposed to it for an extended period. They may lose confidence in their judgments and begin to doubt everything they've ever said or done. Mental and emotional issues might arise as a result of gaslighting. Feelings of uncertainty and insecurity may cause anxiety. Co-dependency, PTSD, and depression are all possible outcomes of such worry.

The long-term consequences of gaslighting may be harmful to the victim. It will take some time for the benefits to take hold, but they will eventually. There are three stages: disbelief, defence, and depressive stage. Let's begin with the impacts of gaslighting before going into the phases.

Confusion

GASLIGHTING works when the victim is unaware of it. The abuser's consistent employment of gaslighting methods might lead to the victim's eventual submission to their will. In time, the victim's uncertainty grows, and the more gaslighting takes place, the victim becomes more perplexed about what is going on. It is clear to the victim, yet they cannot identify the particular issue. Abuse and narcissism may be considered a never-ending cycle for victims as long as they have intimate contact with their abusers. The narcissist preyed on the victim's weaknesses, which led to the muddle. To keep their victims guessing, narcissists can surprise them constantly. One moment they'll do something kind; the next, they'll be harsh.

Intending to destabilise their victims further, the abuser often disassembles them piece by piece. When the victim's bodily and emotional uncertainty becomes too much for them to bear, they turn to them for help and support. Consequently, the victims get isolated since they don't know how the problem came to be in the first place.

Loss of self-belief

The self-esteem of the person who has been gaslighted by a narcissist plummets. As a result, the victim develops self-doubt. Whenever they make a choice, they ask themselves, "What if I...?" If you've been subjected to gaslighting, you've probably begun to live in constant terror of making a mistake. The narcissist's constant blaming, projection, humiliation and falsehoods make you more sensitive. You wonder whether you're being too sensitive while waiting for the narcissist's permission before making any move. When you're acting out of fear, you're more likely to make mistakes in all of your endeavours. As time passes, you, the victim, will begin to display poor self-esteem and self-worth indicators. When someone compliments you, you'll have a hard time saying "thank you." It is the effect of the gaslighter's inflicting emotional harm on the victim.

Negative thoughts about oneself are common among victims because they embrace the narcissist's belief that they are less valuable than they are. A gaslighting victim would avoid eye contact with others because they are frightened that they will see through them and find out their faults if they keep looking. As a result of feeling that you can never do anything right in the eyes of your abuser, you may find yourself apologising all the time. As a way to avoid more humiliation and name-calling, you may also do this. There is a chance that your remarks may make you apologise.

Indecision

If you've been subjected to gaslighting, you've probably questioned everything. Because you, as the victim, will have no notion of what is genuine and what is not. Those subjected to gaslighting may find it difficult to distinguish between right and wrong, even when faced with the most basic of decisions. For victims, even the simplest actions, like cleaning their teeth, are difficult to make. These people become ensnared in the web of narcissism. The narcissist and victim form a close friendship based on the worry that the victim would lose their sense of self. A portion of the victim's psyche will strive to conform to the gaslighter's tastes and requirements, while another part will struggle to maintain their own. In addition, a narcissist may transfer their anxieties about responsibility and perfection onto the victim. Consequently, the general apprehension about accepting responsibility makes it much more difficult to make critical decisions. Indecision

Victims tend to lose their ability to make judgments over time until they have none left. Consequently, the narcissist will have to be their main source of support, and they would have to beg for their approval before doing anything.

Distrust

People who have been manipulated by their minds strive to cover it up because of the embarrassment that they feel. For many people, when their friends and family begin to notice that something is off, they try to cover it up. They may even be able to sidestep the issue completely. Gaslighting victims tend to keep information from others who care about them. When narcissist discovers this, they are afraid of what will happen. They begin to isolate themselves from the rest of the world and distrust others. People subjected to gaslighting find it difficult to trust even close family members and friends, much alone themselves. Distrust prevents sufferers from forming new connections or friendships and instead causes them to withdraw socially and emotionally from those close to them.

Once the gaslighter is gone, the victim still feels the effects of gaslighting. They have difficulty trusting new people when trying to create new friendships. As a result, they tend to be too cautious in their romantic endeavours.

Melancholy

Gaslighting will eventually rob the victim of his or her pleasure and happiness. The victims of narcissists are left confused, terrified, dissatisfied, and lonely as a result of emotional abuse and mental manipulation. The victims are left with the impression that they were once someone else entirely, someone carefree and self-assured. However, they do not grasp the concept that a person's personality might be altered by being exposed to a gaslighter regularly—victims of gaslighting experience a major shift in their personality due to the abuse. Someone who used to be happy, peaceful, and sociable is now unhappy due to mental abuse.

How to survive a gaslighter

On the other hand, the gaslighters have a hard time letting go of the control they have over their surroundings and making the most of what is available to them. When they can't control anything, they put the responsibility on someone else. Gaslighting narcissists are difficult to connect to and work with because of their need for control. Even though you have a solution for every situation, a gaslighter will still attempt to use their arsenal to knock you down and make you accept the responsibility. A narcissist may cause you to feel anxious while you're around them. They tend to invent new methods to get what they want out of a need for power and control. Gaslighting victims need to be aware that they have been victims of this kind of abuse to recover.

Gaslighting may be difficult to deal with since you may have been emotionally damaged. Regaining control of one's life after encountering a gaslighter will take time. Emotional abuse might be difficult to deal with, but it is never impossible. You may accomplish this by discovering new strategies to disarm a narcissist, gaslighting you. A gaslighter may be dealt with in several ways.

Taking a step back from the situation

As the first step in disarming someone who uses gaslighting, you need to regain your vitality. Amid a gaslighter's deceit, you allow yourself to get emotionally depleted. There is no doubt that you are being misled by gaslighting. The gaslighting narcissist will not tolerate any further drama from you. Quit debating with them, don't fall for their falsehoods, don't explain yourself, and remove yourself from the situation completely. Gaslighters are prone to verbal sparring. The reason for this is that they are well-versed in the art of having you respond to what they say. They know when they've pushed you too far, and you're trying to defend yourself vocally. You may put a gaslighter off balance by being cool. The only thing that can make them irrational is your calmness. Keeping your calm will force them to either change their conduct or leave.

Narcissistic gaslighters will slow down and look over their weapons the moment you start paying attention. They'll strive to come back even more ferociously. You can, however, hinder their attempts if you don't give in. As time goes on, they'll learn to keep a safe distance from one another. But don't succumb to the temptation of lowering yourself to their level.

Avoid using the phrase "I'm sorry"

To avoid criticism or harm, you may begin to repeat the phrases of a gaslighter repeatedly in your relationship. You'll have to accept that not saying sorry is an excellent method to deal with someone narcissistic. You may be conscious of apologising for yourself and the narcissist for how you feel and how you feel about them. Apologising for everything you do and don't do has become second nature. You've been apologising for everything that's gone wrong, even though you had nothing to do with it. It is time to stop apologising. By constantly apologising, you're fuelling the gaslighter's belief that they are flawless in their own eyes. All you've done is bolster their determination. The feelings of a gaslighting narcissist can never be your responsibility, no matter what you do. Don't take responsibility for how they're feeling. You need to stop since you will be the one who is accountable for encouraging all of their actions if you don't.

Emotional self-control

Emotional control may be compared to disengaging yourself from circumstances when you suspect a gaslighter is manipulating you by utilising words—an additional tool for dealing with the harsh comments of a gaslighting narcissist. A narcissist's poor conduct will only worsen if they show their feelings. As long as they see that you're in a good mood, they'll keep doing what they're doing! Narcissists' influence will wane as you learn to exercise self-restraint.

Placing your priorities first

It all boils down to being confident in your skin. When dealing with a narcissistic gaslighter, you're more likely to prioritise their wants and needs than your own. You must realise that taking care of yourself is all about doing what you like. The fact that you love yourself does not imply that you are selfish. You hand up control of your life to the narcissist when you attend to his or her wants and desires. In our early years, we are indoctrinated with the idea that being unselfish is a virtue. You may develop the habit of putting others' needs ahead of your own when these tendencies persist into adulthood and become ingrained in your behaviour. However, if you take care of yourself first, a gaslighting narcissist will have fewer opportunities of using you. Prioritise taking care of your own needs.

Gaslighting's debilitating effects might lead you to believe that everything awful that happens to you is your fault. A wicked individual could even be blamed on your shoulders. You don't have to accomplish everything all at once. Instead, make a concerted effort to start small and see if you can make a difference. Try to be considerate of your well-being.

Restoring your identity

Emotional abuse from a gaslighter might cause you to lose your self-esteem. Rebuilding implies that you will have to let go of the old self that was mistreated and controlled. If you can, try to invest in your future self. Spend a certain amount of time each morning envisioning your future self.

You must hang on to your future self while you go on with daily tasks. You'll need to cultivate the notion that you can always improve. There is no longer any need to hold the gaslighting narcissist responsible for your improvement. To be happy, you will have to rely only on your efforts.

4

Seeking validation from others

FOR EVERYONE, it's understandable if they want others to believe in their ideas, choices, accomplishments, or viewpoints. It's very uncommon for children to celebrate their accomplishments by jumping up and down in celebration. As children, we rely on our parents to tell us that we performed a nice deed.

It is the "awareness and acceptance" of someone else's experience that Dr Karen Hall defines as "validation." The capacity to identify and appreciate one's own interior experience is called "self-validation." As long as you can accept the opinions and experiences of others, you'll be able to see their point of view as genuine.

Being interdependent and reliant on the comments and support of others around us is an important aspect of receiving validation. In certain elements of their lives, even the most self-reliant persons need external validation; nevertheless, they may accept their self-validation if they do not get it from someone else.

When self-validation is not feasible or is not appreciated, there is an issue with this. To put it another way, if someone values the opinion, approval, or acknowledgement of others more than they value their own emotions, they will continually seek external validation from that person.

Validation from others

An important part of the urge to be validated by others stems from the way individuals use social media to construct their sense of self and identity based on the reactions of others to their postings. In his book **Social: Why Our Brains Are Wired to Connect**, professor Matthew Lieberman of psychology at the University of California, Los Angeles, discovered that social media satisfies the urge to be a part of a community and prevents one from feeling alone and vulnerable.

For the most part, we all have a buddy who is always posting on social media and constantly checking to see whether their posts are getting the kind of attention they want. Over 3.2 billion individuals across the globe use social media daily, and it's not just a small number. According to Emarsys research, this figure represents around 42 per cent of the entire world population.

The United Kingdom has approximately 70% of adults using Facebook, with 90.4 per cent of Millennials claiming themselves as active users. Increasingly, individuals are using the thumbs up, commenting, or sharing buttons to show their support for one other.

For example, anxiety, despair, and poor self-esteem may result from a need for in-person validation and a need for recognition in all areas of life.

You may have realised exactly how adept you are at making yourself feel down and depressing. As a people-pleaser, you put yourself under a lot of pressure by giving commands, enforcing a tight set of personal rules, and holding yourself to a high bar of unreasonable and judgemental expectations. You do this all to be a nice person!

Abusing 'shoulds'

You need to remove all the 'should' expressions from your vocabulary.

'Should', 'must', 'ought', and 'have-to' infiltrate your mental computer like a virus, destroying your ability to experience contentment, fulfilment, or achievement.

Instead, you've fallen prey to your own mind's relentless pressure and severe judgment, turning you into a victim of totalitarian control. Guilt, shame, blame, discouragement, and melancholy are all possibilities when you don't follow your internal instructions perfectly. As a result of others' failure to live up to your standards, you get enraged, frustrated, disappointed, and even accused.

It is time to stop 'shoulding' and 'must-urbating'

They are all simply recast as preferences. It's more reasonable to say, "I would prefer if people didn't reject me," rather than an injunction against it. Another person may reject you because of their biases or preconceptions rather than your faults, which is also an option.

You may express your choice more rationally if you say, "I would prefer that people, particularly those I love, remain with me and not desert or reject me," rather than effectively forbidding them. It suggests that you have complete control over what other people can and cannot do, which you do not have. This implicit and correct acceptance that others have the freedom to make their own decisions, even if they may disappoint or harm you, is included in the declaration of preference; on the other hand.

Demanding 'should' statements have been identified by Dr David Burns and other practitioners of Cognitive Therapy—a widely used therapy aiming at altering the incorrect thinking that creates unpleasant moods and emotions—as one of the most common errors in patients' thinking. When Cognitive Therapy was introduced in the 1970s, the idea that excessive use of 'should' statement sabotages emotional health and pleasure was not new. Dr Karen Horney originated the phrase "the tyranny of the should" around thirty years earlier to describe the shackling power of personal norms.

The wordplay verb forms should and 'must-urbating' were devised by Dr Albert Ellis, the creator of Rational-Emotive Behaviour Therapy (a precursor of current Cognitive Behaviour Therapy), to depict the poking, damaging influence of personal demands.

People who are "lovely neurotics," in the words of Ellis, are "self-upsetting creatures" who make their lives unpleasant by holding on to three essential musts or shoulds:

1. "I must do well, satisfy others, or be loved by important ones, or I will be useless." (As a result of this urge, melancholy and anxiety take hold).

2. "You must treat me nicely, pleasantly, or appreciatively, otherwise you are wrong and nasty." It's easy to become frustrated and angry when you're forced to follow this rule. If you're a people-pleaser, you could blame yourself for not doing enough to win others' respect or compassion.

3. "Life conditions must or should be the way I want them to be, or it will be dreadful, catastrophic, or disastrous." Anger, fear, uncertainty, and blame are some of the emotions that might result from this mandate.

Humans, according to Ellis, are wired to believe these 'musts' and 'shoulds' because they are founded on strong needs and desires. Rather than the want or need itself, the issue is how it is presented as a need or a demand on how things should be.

It's not realistic to expect other people to love and appreciate you, even if you put yourself in harm's way. However, please get some affection. It would be much better if people liked you for who you are, not just for what you do for them.

Similar to this, you may aspire to be a dependable confidant for others. However, dictating that you never say "no" or let someone down is an overly rigorous rule that you just cannot guarantee in light of life's unforeseen circumstances and requirements. If you're honest with yourself about your desire to be a loyal friend and ally, you're acknowledging the potential that you may need to say "no" sometimes due to circumstances beyond your control or for your survival.

No matter how hard you try, the world will not bend to your will

Expecting things to be a certain way simply leads to disappointment, despair, and many other negative emotions.

Demanding a specific treatment from other people and the world or life prepares you for anger, disappointment, and depression when they don't or can't comply with your will. Demanding unreasonable or unachievable actions or sentiments from yourself can only lead to feelings of shame and inadequacy.

It comes down to this: the only thing you should do is get rid of as many 'shoulds' as you can from your vocabulary. You'll feel better emotionally if you substitute the 'shoulds' with words about what you want, need, or prefer.

Do you give advice or impose your 'shoulds' on others?

Even if you're aware of the strict restrictions you set for yourself, you're not likely to think of yourself as judgemental or critical of others. Your well-intentioned support might easily be misinterpreted as smug disapproval, superiority, harsh criticism or even reprimand if you share your rigorous standards with others in the guise of advice.

Olivia's story

Olivia, 48, is the mother of two married boys and one college-aged daughter. A deep depression she'd felt before the holidays prompted her to seek treatment for the first time in her life. Olivia claims that the family's conversation during their annual Christmas dinner is to blame for her recent mood swings.

Olivia stated that she and her whole family had returned home for the holidays. "We were all sitting down to enjoy the delicious meal I'd made for us. In addition to my sons and their wives, I had two daughters-in-law along with my daughter, husband, and our small granddaughter."

"At dinner, I said that I consider myself to be a nice, welcoming, and tolerant person. Laughter erupted across the household. While everyone else had a good time, I was completely stumped."

"Then I insisted on them telling me what was so amusing about it. My children have said that I am the most judgemental, opinionated, and authoritarian person they have ever met! They often informed me that I was full of 'free advice' that no one wanted to hear. A 'walking talking should machine,' as my daughter put it. 'You should do this,' she said, 'and you should not do that,' to the delight of everyone save my own. Wow, that hurt!"

"Although they were a little more kind, even my daughters-in-law agreed. That was their way of letting me know that they realised I was doing it out of concern and wanted to be supportive and helpful to others. Though I'm sure they're true, both remarked that I make them feel like they don't measure up and that there's no other way to do things. Their husbands—my sons—resent it when I tell them how to make them happy."

Olivia said she was "utterly distraught" at the end of the story. "I didn't know the terrible impact my 'assistance' was having on others. I cherish my relationships with those close to me, both blood relatives and new acquaintances. My husband tells me that I do too much for others all the time. There are occasions when my children or friends get irritated with me, but I've never been able to explain why. In the past, I've thought it was because I wasn't being supportive and helpful enough or that I was being too open about my views. Now, it seems like everything I've done has backfired. I'm in such a bad mood that getting out of bed is almost impossible."

Olivia realised that she had a good heart at this point in treatment, but her techniques were inadequate. When Olivia was a child, she realised that her mother's "useful advise and constructive criticism" was the source of her 'should' rules, which she confessed caused comparable feelings of inadequacy among Olivia and her sisters.

"Even though it was hard, I believe my family gave me the finest Christmas gift of all that night. It was pointed out to me that I was imposing my ideas on others, which is the last thing I want to do to those I care about."

You may be like Olivia in that you want to be there for the

people close to you who are going through difficult times. When you tell people what they should do, you may wind up making them feel like they're doing things incorrectly because they don't do things your way.

There is a risk that you may be too concerned with finding a solution or leaping to the "fix" when others just need you to be empathetic. You may be an excellent sounding board for your friends and family members by listening and providing a secure environment in which they can work through their issues.

The importance of correct reasoning

'Should' statements use hyperbolic language such as 'always,' 'never,' or 'everyone,' which make achieving the unreasonable demands even more difficult and unlikely?

The use of absolute terms and excessive language is a sign of faulty thinking. Depression, anxiety, and other unpleasant mood states are often caused by mistaken thinking. In contrast to your sensations, your ideas might be correct or incorrect. The more correct and sensible your reasoning, the less likely you are to experience emotional distress or bad sensations.

When your self-and other perceptions are true, you'll have a better sense of your inner and outside worlds. This is particularly true when it comes to travelling with other individuals. Accurate ideas allow us to comprehend ourselves and others better; faulty thoughts, on the other hand, cause us to lose our boundaries and become lost in our minds.

The difficulty arises when people-pleasing becomes exaggerated. To cure the 'desire to please,' you need to be selective and modest in how much effort you put into making other people happy.

To ease some of the tension and strain you experience from attempting to achieve such exaggerated time requirements, always replace and never in your people-pleasing thinking with more reasonable language, such as most of the time, occasionally, or rarely.

Your 'shoulds' use also include conditional phrases that relate your expectations about how others should treat you to duties you feel have been generated by your people-pleasing efforts on their behalf. You seem to feel entitlement and perhaps a whiff of manipulation in these conditional regulations.

Suppose, for instance, you were to tell someone, "You must like me because of all the lovely things I do for you." When you state your rules aloud, your coercive nature becomes clear.

A one-sided deal fails unless the other party specifically agrees to like you or treat you well in return for your efforts. It's good to be liked and appreciated by others, but it's not a given, no matter how kind you've been to them.

The only thing you'll get out of holding onto conditional views about how others should treat you is a sense of disappointment, rage, hatred against specific individuals and cynicism about others in general.

In addition, conditional thinking is a trap that confines you to self-blame and remorse. Think about it this way: You can't blame yourself if other people fail to meet your expectations because of your inability to meet theirs.

Voices of the past

In your thoughts or self-talk, you're hearing the judgmental voice of your conscience when you hear the imperative 'should'. Your parents, teachers, elder siblings, coaches or other authority figures have all contributed to that voice, which has remained constant throughout your life because of the restrictions they imposed at different stages.

Even if you've grown out of the need to please other people, your conscience still guides your behaviour. You show that you are prepared to put the demands of others ahead of your own, and you continue to place others in charge over you. Consciousness treats you like a kid, even if you may be caring for others in what seems like a parenting role and completing your adult duties and commitments.

Your conscience offers you a symbolic pat on the back when you follow your strict should standards. Condemnation and guilt are generated when you don't live up to your standards.

Your conscience is double-handedly punishing if you are a people-pleaser. Emotions of humiliation exacerbate your guilt because you judge your performance based on whether others are satisfied with you rather than merely whether you are content with yourself. As with guilt, shame arises when you perceive that others are dissatisfied with your actions.

Even though you're a people-pleaser, you can become harsh when the assault is aimed at yourself. More 'shoulds' and 'shouldn'ts' ("I should have done more," "I shouldn't be angry or resentful," etc.) are common in self-critical monologues, but they're not the only ones.

Labels like "selfish," "self-centred," and "unlovable" may be used to berate and criticise yourself. While your own perceived weaknesses and failings tend to be exaggerated, you will prefer to reduce the severity of others' transgressions and defects. This is a telescopic mental trick.

Perfectionism for the sake of pleasing others

People who have the 'desire to please' are seldom, if ever, completely happy with themselves and their accomplishments. It is common for people-pleasers to seek the favour of others while withholding it from themselves.

Every day, you put forth the extra effort to show your worth to the people around you by doing things for them. It seems that your psychological economy lacks any reserves for positive acts. It doesn't matter how many kind and generous things you've done in the past; you reply now as if your worth is always being re-evaluated with each new request or declaration of need. It's as though you've got nothing to your name as the day begins.

Pervasive feelings of inadequacy, such as nagging doubts and persistent concerns that you haven't done enough, tried hard enough, given enough, or said "yes" enough to satisfy others, drive us to always try to please others.

There is no lack of effort or capacity to satisfy on your side to blame for this disturbing feeling that you're inadequate. Its ultimate cause is the concealed perfectionism that lurks between the lines of your should rules...

"I should satisfy these should and shouldn't expectations of myself totally and perfectly," is the eleventh supplemental commandment. You have two tiers of meticulous standards that you hold yourself to.

First and foremost, you expect yourself always to be able to satisfy everyone else. Second, you require that you always maintain a pleasant emotional state. While trying to please others at the expense of your own needs, you must maintain an enthusiastic and cheerful attitude. You are not allowed to express your bad emotions to anybody, even if you are feeling down.

Self-imposed emotional cruelty is nothing short of holding oneself to exacting standards such as these.

If you think that's over the top, consider if a mother told her kid to satisfy these standards: The mum firmly tells the youngster, *"You must always satisfy me. No matter what you're doing or feeling, you're expected to carry out any orders or requests I give you. All the time, you should be joyful and smile. You will be punished if I ever hear you whine or express any other emotion than joy. I will stop loving you if you don't do these things precisely. Any further concerns?"*

This sounds like the insane speech of a fairy tale villain, such as the nasty stepmother. As an alternative, the speaker may be a narcissistic "Mummy Dearest," who is abusing her kid on an emotional and psychological level that is more realistic. Even if your inner monologue isn't as harsh as that of your "mother," the high expectations and harsh judgments you hold for yourself are eerily similar.

Setting high expectations in many areas of life is not necessarily bad or harmful. On the other hand, trying to achieve perfection is a self-defeating and inescapable recipe for failure. However, striving for perfection is energising since it is a goal that can be achieved in the end.

Attitude modification: The self-destructive 'shoulds' of people-pleasers

Focus on the adjustments below to counteract your self-sabotaging 'shoulds.' Maintaining Albert Ellis's recommendation to quit blaming yourself and others and to avoid 'must-urbating' as much as possible while you do so can help.

It's easy to become stiff and excessive when you're always thinking about what you 'should' or 'must' or 'ought to' do. Flexibility, moderation, and balance are the three hallmarks of rational thinking that will benefit you the most.

It is oppressive and forceful to impose your expectations on others. Instead of using "you should" and "you shouldn't" statements, use sentences such as "I would prefer if...," "It could be better if...," or "I would appreciate it if you..." instead.

You'll do much better if you set more achievable and reasonable expectations for how you'd want to be treated and how others should treat you.

Don't worry about doing everything perfectly, even if it means pleasing people or having a happy outlook on life. Perfection is an unattainable goal. It's energising to strive for perfection.

5

Not being nice is alright

IT WOULD BE LOVELY if you had to sum up a people-pleaser in one word. Nice isn't only a personality trait if you suffer from the 'desire to please.' Behaving nicely is an abbreviation for a belief system that defines how one should interact with others to avoid negative outcomes.

However, the formula isn't always successful. As you surely already know, bad things happen to good people. Even though they may not be deserving of it, kind and generous individuals are often mistreated by others. In addition, lovely individuals are often plagued by self-imposed emotional burdens such as anxiety, despair, and even panic attacks because of their good character.

Isabella's story

At the age of nine, Isabella was told by her doctor that her mother had breast cancer. She vividly remembers her talk with her father and her mother's doctor about the need of keeping her mother happy and stress-free for her to recover. Afraid to see her mother's death, Isabella was convinced that her mother's life hinged on Isabella's conduct as a decent and pleasant child.

Isabella had been severely disciplined by her teacher for taunting and making fun of a handicapped student on the school playground a few weeks before detecting a lump in her mother's breast. According to the letter, the instructor demanded to meet with Isabella's parents to discuss their daughter's conduct at the school.

With tears in her eyes, her mother pleaded with her daughter, "We've tried to educate you to be a decent person and polite to everyone. In light of this revelation, I am shocked and disgusted by what you did to the young girl in the wheelchair." In the end, she said, "Your father and I are ashamed of you."

When Isabella was punished for not being courteous to the young girl, she was ordered to remain indoors for a week and reflect on how much she had hurt her. Isabella's parents asked her to write three letters of apology: One for their disappointment, one for the parents of the disabled kid, and a third for herself.

Isabella expressed her regret and remorse in her letters for "not being polite" and "hurting the other girl's emotions." A commitment to never again be cruel or harsh to anybody was something she made to herself and her parents. Isabella distinctly remembers a strong sense of sorrow and guilt.

Isabella promised herself during her mother's illness: if she survived, she would always be a good kid. As long as she didn't die, she vowed to never be nasty or teased to anybody again, particularly her little brother.

Isabella's mother was fortunate enough to make it out alive. Isabella, on the other hand, became a master at pleasing others. The belief that being good may prevent unpleasant things from occurring to Isabella remained even as she grew older. She feared severe repercussions if she ever said an unkind word or acted irrationally toward her family, friends, or workers.

Regardless of Isabella's outbursts, most people-pleasers cling to the belief that they are lovely people. People-pleasers can't say or do anything nasty because of their inherent niceness, regardless of what others say or do to them. People-pleasers are sometimes unable to admit to themselves that they have unpleasant sentiments about others.

However, there is a big cost to being polite that you should no longer be prepared to pay. When you can say, "It's acceptable not to be pleasant," you've taken a huge step in curing yourself of your 'desire to please.'

Take the quiz below to see how much of your present thinking is motivated by a desire to be kind.

Quiz

Consider each statement to see if it applies to your situation.

1. I take satisfaction because I am a good person. **True or False**

2. It is tough for me to reject another person, no matter how much she or he may deserve it.
True or False

3. I probably go too far in doing good things for others.
True or False

4. It is much simpler for me to admit unpleasant sentiments about myself than it is to communicate unfavourable feelings about others.
True or False

5. When anything goes wrong, I often blame myself.
True or False

6: I feel that I should always be courteous.
True or False

7. I may do too much for people, be too kind, or even allow myself to be exploited to avoid rejection for other reasons.
True or False

8. I feel that those who are pleasant get the approval, love, and friendship of others.
True or False

9. I don't believe it's appropriate to get angry at others.

True or False

10. I should not be angry or unhappy with the people I care about.
True or False

11. I'm terrified of being ignored, rejected, or even punished if I'm not kind to others.
True or False

12. Even if people take advantage of my good nature, I feel I should always be kind.
True or False

13. I shield myself from rejection, condemnation, and abandonment by being polite and doing things to satisfy people.
True or False

14. I don't consider myself a kind person if I criticise others, even if they deserve it.
True or False

15. I strive to be a good person to get others to like me.
True or False

16. At times, I feel as if I need to "purchase" other people's affection and friendship by doing pleasant things for them.
True or False

17. Being kind often hinders me from voicing unpleasant thoughts toward people.
True or False

18. I feel people would characterise me as nice, charming, and agreeable.
True or False

19. I believe my friends should like me because of all the great things I do for them.
True or False

20. I want everyone to think of me as a pleasant person.
True or False

A step-by-step Guide for evaluating your answers

For each question, count the number of times you marked "True" as your answer.

Anywhere **from 14 to 20** is considered "too nice" under this test's scoring system. Despite your best efforts, your interpersonal connections and emotional well-being may probably suffer. You're paying a hefty price for being a good sport. The pace of your rehabilitation will increase if you replace negative attributes in your fundamental self-concept with positive ones.

You may have people-pleasing issues if your score falls **between 8 and 13**, which is indicative of a tendency to put others before yourself. You'll get well faster if you let go of your rosy self-perception.

A score **between 5 and 7** indicates that although you're still concerned about how others see you, you're less concerned than most people-pleasers. Remember that being kind isn't one of your skills. Meanwhile, you should keep an eye on your tendency to be kind at your own cost and keep a tight eye on your psychological surroundings.

A score of **0 to 4** indicates an exceptionally low level of care for being nice for someone with the 'desire to please.' Denial is a common pitfall, so be sure you're not falling into it. To be honest, if you've successfully overcome the urge to be nice only for the sake of it, you've already gone a long way. Make the most of what you've got.

Being "nice"

People's personalities are considerably more intriguing and complex than you may think. The fact that a person's personality traits are ascribed to them at an early age and form a fundamental component of their self-concept means that the label will major influence their ideas, emotions, and behaviour throughout their lives.

A well-behaved child is often referred to as "nice" by adults such as parents, teachers, and priests. It's common to hear, "What a wonderful young girl you are!" or "There's a nice boy." These words and phrases may be familiar to you.

"Nice" is also prescriptive by parents and other prominent adults, as in, "You should be nice," since it connotes being courteous and well-mannered. "Nice girls don't go to bars," or "Nice ladies don't 'go all the way,'" are examples of proscriptive phrases used to distinguish morally sound activities from immoral or amoral ones.

It's interesting to notice how frequently the quality of "niceness" is dismissed and even disparaged when attributed to grownups. "She's nice, but..." or "He's a good man, but..." are both examples of subjective phrases followed by qualifiers. The discounting, however, often indicates a negative character trait.

'Nice' is defined as pleasant or delightful in dictionaries. If you're a kind person, you're more likely to be seen as flat rather than three-dimensional. They don't have a lot of sharp edges or distinct personality traits. Nice people don't create waves in groups or organisations. And although they don't offend anybody, pleasant people don't get the attention they deserve either. Because the villains were "far more intriguing," my daughter once said that she preferred the villains over the heroes because they were "more engaging."

The exact attributes of compliance, ingratiation and agreeability that are often linked with their defining feature are disparaged in certain circles against good people. This subtle but unfavourable reaction to niceness is captured in Jane Austen's portrayal of a female character in one of her stories:

"Since she was nothing more than a nice and obedient young lady, we had no reason to dislike her—she was just disliked."

Understandably, your self-image as a people-pleaser is based on the fact that "nice" equals "pleasing." If being pleasant is a character attribute and a source of self-esteem that is at best ambiguous, why does it seem so appealing as a rule of thumb? What is it about activities at odds with good that causes us such stress and worry?

Using kindness as a form of emotional defence

As a people-pleaser, you need to recognise the benefits of being nice as a form of self-protection. In the context of interpersonal protection, being kind has a far greater value than just being a good person.

According to people-pleasers, avoiding unpleasant experiences such as rejection, abandonment, disapproval, and rage may be achieved by being kind. The other passengers should not want to throw you off if you don't produce any waves or disturb the boat.

On the other hand, people-pleasers often go above and beyond to make sure that others see them not just as normally kind but as unusually so. On the other hand, people-pleasers frequently go to great measures to show their care and regard. Since no one would want to attack you if you are so kind and generous to others, being too nice might provide a false sense of security.

Consider your answers to statements 7, 8, 11, 13, 15, 16, and 19 from the quiz you took earlier in this chapter. If you can identify yourself with at least some of these assertions, you're employing niceness as a type of interpersonal protection. According to your answers to these seven questions, you believe that being kind to others will lead to reciprocation in the form of appreciation, love, and acceptance on your part. Your niceness and the goodwill it generates protect you from being rejected, abandoned, disapproved of, or otherwise emotionally damaged.

Initially, it looks to be a rational and sensible position. Even the great scientist-philosopher Dr Hans Selye, the father of contemporary ideas such as stress and stress-induced disease, approved this view. As Selye put it, the greatest defence against interpersonal stress is to be kind and helpful to others. Selye had this view because he thought that the tension that comes from being with other people was harmful.

"Altruistic egoism" was Selye's term for stress management. According to this saying, when you do good deeds for others, you're truly behaving in your self-interest. Selye stated that if you are nice and kind to others, they will reciprocate, and you will be less likely to experience stress.

So, what are the differences between people-pleasers notion of niceness-as-protection and Dr Selye's sensible advice on altruistic egoism? It was clear to Dr Selye that being kind wouldn't keep you safe from everyone all the time. To him, it didn't matter how well you treated someone; they could still do you emotional pain, no matter how well you treated them. There are several reasons why this might happen, including the fact that the other person is inherently hateful, prejudiced, or bigoted, or that he or she has a grudge against you and wants to make things right by punishing you, or that the other person is simply not emotionally healthy or mature enough to be loved and to love in return.

People-pleasers, on the other hand, take kindness as a creed. They believe that being polite has magical powers that prevent others from being rude or hurtful. According to people-pleasing reasoning, if niceness fails to prevent an interpersonal insult or injury, you must be more pleasant!

The "magical" thoughts you've had in the past?

Children's magical thinking is the foundation of this pervasive but erroneous notion that being kind can save you from harm. It's a mentality where ideas and actions are indistinguishable, known as magical thinking. As a result, thoughts have the same impact as actions.

Of course, if this were true, it would provide magical abilities to everybody who could think. A single desire is all it takes to come true in a child's mind.

Magical thinking is common among young children, who

employ it to fend off their anxieties. To retain the appearance of control, children establish conditional agreements in their heads. "If I go to sleep and leave the lights on, you can't come out or harm me," a child would tell imagined creatures in his or her closet.

If a kid believes that his or her parents will not divorce if he or she is nice and does all they ask of him or her, he or she may attempt to negotiate for this to happen. A child's collection of magical circumstances that guarantee protection from danger might easily integrate "being kind."

Age 7 to 8 in normal development is when kids realise that there is a difference between thinking and acting, between wanting and making something happen in the here-and-now. When a child reaches adolescence, the vast majority of their magical fantasies have evolved into concrete intentions and actions, including faith and prayer, that are socially acceptable.

There are, however, certain infantile ways of thinking—some magical thoughts—that might remain with you throughout your life. As a result, they may last for decades if they help alleviate fear and anxiety. You may conclude that they don't influence you if you view them in the harsh light of grown-up reality and reasoning. Despite this, you cling to their promise of protection.

For those who still believe in the power of kindness to shield them from harm, this may be a remnant of their magical childhood thinking. Depression and emotional suffering may result from feeling rejected, abandoned, or alone. These "monsters" need to be contained. Reality-based anxieties like the imagined occupants of a child's closet, on the other hand, are not fantasy-based worries like those of a child's closet.

Do you still experience "magical" thoughts?

Even for kids, the link between good behaviour and avoiding terrible consequences is not merely mystical; it is based on fact. It's common for kids to learn through direct experience that if they follow their parents' wishes and regulations, they will be rewarded with praise and/or avoid punishment. On the other hand, children are frequently shown that if they violate rules or defy parental or school authority, they will be penalised and disciplined. Behaving kindly stops at least some negative things from occurring in a real way.

Adding magical thinking and childlike omnipotence to the real foundation of niceness is common among young children. This implies that being pleasant may be seen as having the capacity to ward off negative repercussions that are beyond the child's control. To avoid the parents' divorce, a youngster like this can promise in his or her head that they will treat each other with respect.

As we saw previously in the example of Isabella, when a particularly disruptive, unpleasant, or traumatic early life event is linked with a belief in the protecting power of niceness, it may have long-lasting consequences. This is particularly true if being pleasant is associated in a child's consciousness with the real avoidance or amelioration of a negative experience. Conversely, acting or thinking anything that was not nice is related to the incidence of trauma.

Even when the stakes are enormous, it is natural to want to re-establish some sense of control in the face of overwhelming stress. Under such circumstances, a kid could deal with a higher power promising to "be nice" and "good" to affect the result of an illness or accident.

Isabella made the link in therapy between saving her mother's life and being pleasant. She realised that her previous "magical thinking" generated the instant worry that something horrible would happen if she wasn't pleasant to someone.

Isabella's situation serves as a powerful example of the psychological benefits of being kind. Isabella's youthful imagination saw her mother's survival as a reward for her commitment to always be nice. That led Isabella to believe that being pleasant was a necessity in a manner that was ultimately self-defeating.

Isabella, who was known for her capacity to always be kind, could not healthily communicate her frustrations. Even though she was aware that people were taking advantage of her kind nature, Isabella was helpless to do something about it. To say "no" or establish any boundaries "wouldn't be kind" to Isabella, who was tired and drained from her people-pleasing attempts.

A positive result, Isabella's mother's survival, is related to Isabella's desire to be kind. Traumatic events may lead to undesirable effects in certain situations. Accidents may cause a parent to die or a sibling to be permanently crippled. It's possible for parents to be divorced, no matter how much their children feel like they have to keep them together.

Despite their childhood tragedies ending in heartbreak, people-pleasers are compelled to be polite in adulthood. Others believe that by being kind, they will be able to prevent terrible things from occurring. Sadly, some people-pleasers carry their childhood guilt through into adulthood, believing that if they had been kinder and better kids, the tragic events would never have occurred.

The 'desire to please' virus starts to spread in infancy for chronic, long-term people-pleasers, and they may not even know it.

In other words, magical or superstitious thinking is erroneous by definition. Rejecting the idea that your niceness can or should keep you safe from the pain of rejection or other bad life experiences is a burden on your attitude and actions. Not only is it unrealistic to expect people to constantly be kind to one another, but it's also not necessarily the right thing to do.

It's good not to be kind

Bad things happen to good people when they're unlucky. Niceness, on the surface, seems to be an innocuous notion, but it is a cognitive minefield.

No matter how strongly you believe in niceness's ability to shield you from harm, the evidence shows that it does not work. It doesn't matter if you're the nicest person on the planet; someone will dislike you because of it.

No matter how polite you are, there are no assurances that you will be rejected, humiliated, ostracised, disapproved of, or even abandoned by other people. You're more likely to be rejected by someone biased towards you because of your colour, ethnicity, gender, or sexual orientation. It doesn't matter how wonderful you are compared to everyone else. Someone else may take a position against you, no matter how much you've helped her. It's not fair, but neither is life.

Review your beliefs on the fairness of life and see whether you still hold them. Having the conviction that being pleasant would shield you from being hurt by others stems from a fundamental belief that life is fair.

Nice individuals like you confront a problem because when things don't go as planned and other people harm you despite your good intentions, you are inclined to get irritated and confused. In addition to frustration, you may get angry if the way people should treat you as a result of your good manners isn't followed through. Of course, you're too good to lash out against those who may have harmed you. Instead, you're more than likely to blame yourself for not being pleasant enough or for some other cause for the maltreatment you've received from others. That way, you'll be able to maintain a sense of fairness in your life. Depression, on the other hand, is the price you'll pay for venting your anger on yourself.

Consider that for a moment. Only pleasant things will happen to decent people in a fair world because they are deserving of happiness. Things would be different if life were more equitable since only unpleasant things would befall good people.

Here's the reality check: even good people like you may suffer bad things.

To avoid self-blame and sadness when awful things happen, you must feel that life is fair and that niceness should shield you from unpleasant things.

Some dangerous yet tempting syllogisms or erroneous logic lurks under the notion that being polite should shield you from being injured by other people. Depressing and self-defeating conclusions follow from the erroneous reasoning:

- Those who deserve it will get it if the world is fair.
- Something horrible occurred to me (e.g., rejection, desertion).
- As a result, I deserve it.

or

- If I'm friendly, no one will reject or harm me.
- I've been rejected and hurt.
- As a result, I'm not as kind as I believe I am or not nice enough.

It's easy to become caught up in a negative cycle of feelings and thoughts. The sickness to please is a self-perpetuating loop fuelled by your need to please and be liked by everyone else.

To combat this depressing style of thinking, it's important to challenge the underlying notion that life is fair. It's certain that when life hands you a painful blow, you'll feel guilty, blamed, and depressed if you cling to the false assumption that being kind would shield you from negative emotions. Keep in mind that changing one's thinking in the triangle of 'desire to please' will break the loop and bring you to healing.

Don't acknowledge abusive treatment

It's possible that being kind might help you win over someone who treats you badly. However, being nice is the weakest link in the chain in this situation.

When someone is emotionally harming you, being pleasant is not a suitable reaction. Being courteous to someone who's using you as a verbal punching bag simply encourages that person to continue to abuse you in the same way. As a result, being kind gives the other person permission to abuse you—and even encourages it!

Being nice all the time puts you at risk for emotionally abusive relationships because you avoid disagreement or confrontation at all costs, and you surrender to the whim of critical and controlling partners or employers.

Even if the assault is one-sided, people-pleasing equals unilateral psychological disarmament in a conflict scenario. A lack of self-defence and an unacceptable level of vulnerability result from being kind while being attacked.

Being kind doesn't work as a defence against abuse, it instead empowers the one who is doing the damage or treating you unfairly.

People-pleasing does not lead to other people abusing you in the first place. The abuser's mentality and life experiences are to blame for these factors. For example, studies demonstrate that abused children grow up to be violent adults.

However, even if you aren't to blame for the treatment you're receiving, your tendency to be kind and amiable is a certain way to perpetuate the cycle of abuse. You may believe that by making an extra effort to satisfy someone who is being disrespectful to you, you are doing something to break the cycle of cruelty. You're doing the exact opposite of what you're supposed to be doing.

Hopeful that the other person's conduct would ultimately be changed by your good deeds, compassion, and love may be a futile endeavour. Sadly, despite your best intentions, this tactic rarely succeeds. As a result, the abuser will just get more confident, and your self-esteem will suffer as a result. You may start to feel that you are entitled to a difficult or abusive environment in the long run.

Of course, your basic human right to be treated with dignity and courtesy must be learned. You must first overcome your erroneous assumption that being kind would shield you from bad treatment or help you triumph over it.

6

Staying in toxic relationships with friends, partners and parents

As was said after the last chapter, there will be some bumps in the road, but this is perfectly acceptable. Isn't it an indication that you haven't overcome your people-pleasing habit or that you'll never be able to say no? This is going to be a long and winding road to learning. There will be a lot of great and a few terrible experiences, but they all have the potential to teach you something.

People's responses to what you say might be rather varied. You can perceive astonishment or pleasure that you are defending yourself. Other people may be upset or disappointed if they don't enjoy your newfound capacity to put yourself first.

A lot of effort will be spent anticipating how the other person will respond before you even say no. Think about it, and you'll start to feel uneasy and perhaps question your choice. The more time you spend worrying about what other people may think, the more anxious you get. Anxiety feeds into our food and sleeping patterns, among other things, and creates a vicious cycle.

Anxiety may be harmful and even deadly. When we start to worry about other people's responses, we'll take a little time to investigate the anxiety we feel.

How to stop worrying about what other people think and remain calm

Trying to satisfy everyone can only lead to disappointment since you will never be able to please everyone. Assume you have to present in front of a group of twenty individuals. Due to your selection, someone will be envious of your success. While one person could make fun of your clothes, the person next to you might think it's perfect. Others give you a warm grin. You may expect a range of responses to any given event. It's possible to obtain more than one out of a single conversation.

Imagine a manager who tells you, "I'm disappointed, but I understand." People-pleasers don't see this as a victory; instead, they see it as evidence that they have let someone down. Although we are not responsible for other people's sentiments and behaviours, we should not feel guilty for our feelings, just as our feelings are our responsibility.

Steps to overcome anxiety over "what others think"

1. Keep a close eye on the situation

When we have to say no, we begin to feel anxious. The next step is to figure out which individuals are more likely to make you feel this way than others. Anxiety might be raised to a greater degree by your closest friend than by your co-worker. Decide on how much control this individual has over you. Your employer may have considerable power because they influence your professional future. Your co-worker, on the other hand, is powerless in your presence. You'll be able to figure out the ideal strategy to concentrate your thoughts by answering these questions.

2. Determine if your concerns are justified

You'll be able to predict how individuals will respond based on your previous interactions with them. If we create up a vision in our heads of how things will come out, it's often not justified. Although it has never happened before, we are afraid that our mother would lose her mind if we didn't attend the family dinner.

Anxiety might be exacerbated when we overestimate the severity of a situation. Even if you have never met the individual before, it's important not to assume that their response will be negative.

3. Consider why you are concerned about the other person's response

You care so much because you want to be liked and respected by others. But what if saying yes doesn't make this person appreciate you or even like you? Consequently, you'll be forced to do something you don't want to do, and the other person won't feel any better about it.

No matter how highly regarded this person thinks of your ability to agree with them, others may argue that this is a steep price to pay for gaining their respect.

4. Recognise the source of your worry

Feeling out of control is a common cause of anxiety and concern. As with feelings, you do not influence how other people perceive your character.

If a person does not like you, you can't change their mind despite your best attempts.

"No, I don't need this person's approval." Isn't there a plethora of other individuals in the world that we can like and who can like us for who we are?

If your worry stems from a sense of helplessness, it's time to reclaim some of that power. The greatest approach to take charge in this circumstance is to walk away.

How to remain calm in the face of anxiety

It's usually better to deal with your anxiety before attempting to say no since doing so will just heighten the tension already there. As soon as the terror sets in, there are a few things you may do to remain calm.

One of the first things you can do when feeling worried is to stand up straight. We feel better because we're taking care of our hearts and lungs. You'll have more self-control if you stand up or sit upright.

Not just deep breathing but taking the same amount of time to inhale and exhale can help you relax. Your mind will be engaged, and you won't be able to think about what has made you anxious.

Try switching things up if you're stuck in a rut because of worry at work. Taking a break from your thoughts might be as simple as grabbing a piece of fruit or using the photocopier.

Avoid sugar. While chocolate maybe your favourite comfort food, the sugar surge it causes might exacerbate your anxiety. Instead, go for a protein-heavy meal, which releases energy more slowly.

Staying calm and preventing anxiety is possible in a variety of ways. Reading a book, watching a humorous video, or going for a stroll are all ways to take your mind off of problems. Another option is to speak with a buddy on the phone. You may open up to them about how you're feeling and then shift the conversation to something constructive, like making a long term plan.

When people get frustrated, here's what to do

It may be unpleasant when someone becomes angry because you said no to their request. You are in pain, but you only have power over your thoughts and feelings. Nevertheless, you have options for improving the issue.

A quick fix to the other person's frustration is to just say yes. However, this is far from the optimal answer.

To avoid the frustrated individual becoming enraged, we must use the following strategies to maintain our values and boundaries without giving in or allowing them to be violated.

Set up a connection with the individual

Avoid statements like "I know how you feel," since they invite responses like "Well if you know how I feel, why don't you simply do it?" It's more about a subliminal connection here. When you replicate the other person's behaviours (such as getting up if they are), you help them form a connection to you.

Take note of what they have to say

Even if you've declined their offer, the exchange isn't over yet. Make an effort to explore whether there is room for compromise. If you can't understand what they're saying, try to repeat it back to them. When they realise they have been heard, they will be able to relax.

Solicit questions

Questions are a sign of interest in finding a solution, and the other person is likely irritated because they can't think of an answer. It's a kind of brainstorming, and it will help them forget that you've turned them down.

Recommend another time to deal with the problem

It may be best for both parties to move away from the situation but not ignore it. "What about an hour? I'll get back to you with some suggestions." Taking a break will allow them to cool down while you brainstorm solutions that won't put you in an awkward position.

People-pleasers rarely become angry or upset because we're always thinking of methods to keep things calm. However, if you begin to employ your soothing tactics while they are agitated, you may make the problem worse. Keep a cool head and be realistic, but don't be abrasive. Your character will improve with time, despite how it may seem now.

Take action to end the use of manipulation methods

"Social influence" is a term used to describe an important aspect of effective interpersonal interactions. It's when one partner in a relationship affects the other as a result of the reciprocal impact. Going to a party just because everyone else is doing so is an example of this.

When it comes to manipulating others, one individual will always have the upper hand. The problem comes when we cannot distinguish between social influence and manipulative behaviour. Our desire to make others happy may cause us to ignore the boundary and only hope that we may make someone else happy.

Before you can stop being controlled, you must first learn to recognise when you are being misled. As a manipulator, you must have the following personality traits:

- Manipulators have a long and complicated history of personal issues. As a result, they'll be both hot and chilly. They may be angelic at one point and evil at another.
- They are masters in identifying a person's flaws.
- They will use every vulnerability they can discover in you to their advantage.
- They can persuade you to give up something to help them.
- They will continue to manipulate you until you force them to change their conduct.
- Manipulators can use your feelings of guilt and the need to please.

Upon identifying a manipulator, you have several alternatives to choose from. The first step is to maintain a safe distance between you and them. People's excessive emotions aren't going to assist your emotional well-being.

When dealing with manipulators, make sure you're in a place where others are present to help you out. When there are witnesses, manipulators are less likely to take advantage of you. If they get angry or confrontational, you will be in a safe area. Recording any improper conduct is a good idea in certain cases.

If you follow this instruction, it's easy to cope with manipulation tactics.

Make sure to remember your boundaries and that you have the right to express your thoughts and ideas, prioritise your own needs, and say no without feeling guilty.

You'll have to be more strong with your no since manipulators don't respect your boundaries. Be cordial, but don't feel the need to apologise. Keep your shoulders back and keep your gaze fixed on the target.

Let them know what you think of their request. Ask them whether they believe your request is reasonable or fair. It's a good idea to find out what you'll gain and whether or not you have any say in the matter. If you put the emphasis back on them, they will probably realise you are aware of what they are doing, even if they are completely aware that they are influencing you.

Keep your head out of the sand and avoid blaming yourself for the circumstance. As a result, ask yourself if this person respects you, whether there is mutual respect in your relationship, and if their requirements are reasonable.

Respond slowly if you need more time. By saying "I'll think about it," or anything similar, you can step back and reflect on how you are being treated.

Manipulators take advantage of our desire to make others happy. They know that we're not pleased, yet we'll go through with it... Not the same as a good friend, whose motives may be for our advantage, such as urging us to dine out at an unfamiliar eatery. The restaurant owner wants your support. Thus the manipulator will employ ways to persuade you to eat there even if you know the cuisine is horrible.

Despite our best efforts, manipulators will continue to infiltrate our lives. Because of this, we must develop the skills necessary to recognise them and put an end to their influence.

Managing obtrusive people

What you choose to do with your time and energy, how you choose to act and behave, is your own business. Unfortunately, many in the world are unable to distinguish between their work and personal life. You might label them as invasive, inquisitive, or even just "busybodies," but the fact remains that they are invading your personal space.

There is no need to fear intrusive individuals since they are rarely hostile and do not want to control you. However, if you reply no, they are more likely to inquire about your reasoning behind the decision. There is a chance that they believe they have the greatest option for you in their mind. As an illustration of invasive conduct, consider these cases:

- Even though you haven't seen your third cousin in years and never really liked her, your parents insist that you attend her wedding. Your parents want to know whether there is anything else more significant going on behind your answer of no.

- Your employer wants you to take on more responsibilities, but you're already overburdened. There's no way you can organise your time in this manner, yet they keep trying.

- Your buddy wants to match you up with someone they are certain you would like.

Avoid feeling compelled to explain why you don't want to do anything when confronted with a circumstance like the one described above. It is sufficient to say, "I have plans" or "I am unavailable." If you prefer, provide alternatives before changing the topic.

A guide to dealing with obtrusive strangers

Depending on the parameters you've selected, some individuals find even the most basic questions invasive when you don't know them well. Try to avoid saying words like "Mind your own business" when someone asks you a question about anything personal. Even if you don't feel like answering a question, there are still methods to reply to it.

Make light of the situation. If someone asks how old you are, tell them you are young.

Inform individuals that you are uncomfortable with certain questions: "I'm not comfortable talking politics."

"I'd want to know more about you," return the discussion to them.

Figure out why they ask these questions. A good way to find out where someone heard about your trip to France is to ask them how they heard about it. You may discover that you have a mutual buddy and therefore feel more at ease discussing the subject.

If someone asks you a question repeatedly, don't be afraid to tell them how you feel. Let the individual know if you are feeling pushed or uncomfortable.

Consider that each of our replies begins with the pronoun "I." For a variety of reasons, this is a desirable habit to cultivate. In the first place, it gives people a better understanding of their boundaries.

As an added benefit, it allows you to take responsibility for how you feel about such inquiries. "It's disrespectful to ask someone their age," on the other hand, does not convey the message that you are uncomfortable. Instead, you are only saying what is socially acceptable or unacceptable.

Even though it may seem like we've gone over the same ground before, remembering that other people's responses are not something you can control or feel guilty about is essential when learning to cope with them. When dealing with the emotions of others, it is important to let them know where your boundaries lie. It also helps if you can stay cool and firm and employ the suggested tactics to bring about a feeling of serenity.

The best ways to make and keep friends and have a meaningful social life

A friend may play a huge influence in your life. They may serve as a bridge between your earliest memories and the people you grew up with later in life. Whether you need a shoulder to cry on or someone to laugh with, your friends are there for you.

Those that are your true friends will be able to correct you without making you feel hurt. They'll also advise you when it's time to stand up for what you believe in. Those who know you best may give you sound advice on how to live your life to the fullest, but they shouldn't take control of your decisions for you.

As a teenager, you assumed your high school pals would be there for you for the rest of your life. Or what if the size of your social network determined your level of success? At this crucial age, many people develop a need to be liked.

As friendships change as we get older and mature, they are still important to us. It's possible that our paths diverge or just grow apart, paving the door for new companions to enter our lives.

A detailed examination of your present connections may have shown that not everyone deserves to be called a friend. Perhaps they didn't appreciate the fact that you've learnt to let go of guilt and the desire to please others, or, worse, that you've identified those who are manipulating you for their advantage. Don't be concerned. Every new experience gives us a chance to meet new people, and maybe this time; you'll meet people who appreciate and value who you are as a person.

Developing the confidence to express yourself proudly

This is a significant accomplishment. New limits and objectives for happiness have given you a renewed sense of purpose and optimism about your life. People are drawn to you like moths to a flame when you're positive. Making new friends is much simpler now that you're a better version of yourself.

First, you need to think about how you might convey your new viewpoint and creativity to others. Now that you've figured out who you are let's work on honing your uniqueness so that you're not tempted to compromise it in the future to please others.

It's not enough to just say what you think. That's why it's good to voice your thoughts, but be careful not to get too opinionated if you don't know what you're protecting. If you've never attempted to learn the Chinese language, you can't discuss how tough it is. It's important to keep in mind that although you have the right to your viewpoint, others also do. Even if you and a buddy can't agree on everything, it doesn't imply your relationship won't last.

This is a great moment to share the unique experiences you've had in your life with others. Even the experiences that made you feel uncomfortable, such as social faux pas, have shaped you into the person you are now. Meeting new individuals is an opportunity to revel in this accomplishment.

The way you look has a bearing on your ability to develop innovative ideas. Just think about how much time you've wasted not wearing the distressed jeans and boots you've always wanted to wear instead. Take pleasure in your appearance by getting the hairstyle and clothing that make you feel good. It doesn't matter what other people think about you; what matters is how you feel about yourself.

When you speak confidently, you will be a role model for people to emulate. They will see how freeing it has been for you and will begin to feel more confident in doing the same. You'll find yourself in demand as a style icon overnight!

All of your thoughts, feelings, and opinions are welcome here. You are not causing any harm to anybody. Some folks may be surprised by your thoughts and viewpoints. If someone disagrees with you, you may feel uncomfortable, but nothing bad will happen.

As soon as you begin to express yourself, some people may be surprised. Your new normal is their job, and it's up to them to adjust to the new you.

You must speak out if you want your voice to be heard. Don't allow the opportunity to express yourself to pass you by and then feel bitter that you didn't.

Consider yourself lucky if you don't always get it right. The inability to articulate one's thoughts and feelings is a common occurrence. Regain mental clarity by concentrating on what you want to say or accomplish.

Get started one step at a time. The more confident you get, the more you can speak your mind in groups, with strangers, and with confident people.

How can I confidently express my opinions?

The first step is to be confident in your thoughts and beliefs. If you want to express your views on the current situation in the world, the first thing you need to do is verify your facts. You may start by writing down a few thoughts and then watch several videos of others discussing the same issue and pay attention to their attitude.

Take a look at the material with a buddy after you're certain you've learned all there is to know about it. Write down what went well and what needs improvement from the dialogue, and then go back to the drawing board for more research if needed.

Making the scenario more difficult for yourself is a great way to improve your practice skills. Next time, invite two or three friends, then the whole family. The more you challenge yourself, the more confident you will be in expressing your thoughts and ideas.

How to make friends without people-pleasing

It's now possible to have equal connections with individuals you meet with which you both share your feelings. To have a connection, you don't have to agree with everything your buddy says, but you recognise it's OK for individuals to have their ideas. You don't have to have the same interests. You need to set your boundaries and respect in the early phases. Here are some of the best methods to make new acquaintances without worrying about pleasing everyone.

- Start a discussion. It's a terrific show of self-assurance, and it may help you get over your first feelings of shyness much more quickly.

- Smiling and showing genuine interest in what others say will go a long way.
- Try to stay away from potentially divisive subjects like politics and religion for the time being.
- Inquire about new things that aren't out of bounds. In other words, if you don't mind being quizzed on these topics, then others probably won't either. This is an excellent approach to introducing new subjects.
- Find out what you have in common with each other. Even if you've been to various cities, these places have a lot in common. Both artists performed at the same show, so it doesn't matter whether you like them or not.
- Focus on open body language, such as not crossing your legs but crossing your feet, and avoid keeping your hands behind your back.
- Find methods to appreciate and make others feel more at ease instead of making judgements about others.
- Kindness is a virtue. You may better understand people's feelings by demonstrating empathy and paying attention when they speak.
- Be the one who is always optimistic. "It's easy to concentrate on the unpleasant parts of today's environment, yet there are also many wonderful things to discuss." Optimism is contagious, so cultivate it in yourself and others.
- Make no comparisons between yourself and your new pals. They may have a college degree, and you do not, or you may have affluent parents who do not value their uniqueness the way you do.
- Make a plan and follow through on it. Suggest a coffee or drink for the next meeting. Keep things low-key until you get to know each other's interests.

We may sometimes go a bit crazy when we're anxious to make friends, especially if we've just discovered our new identity. Rather, we fail because we try too hard to please others rather than be unique. Our social experiment is about to begin, and we can't wait to see the results. People will either love or hate us for who we are, and we don't need to worry about impressing them. Your inherent charisma will wow those around you.

Finally, believe in your new friendships. We may be blaming ourselves for putting our faith in people we later found out were not trustworthy since we've been burned before. However, this is a past matter, and we can do nothing about it now. As long as you're able to defend yourself, you should trust your new friends since they haven't done anything to make you doubt them.

How to develop a lifetime relationship

There are strong foundations for your new connections, such as trust and respect. These bonds must now be strengthened to face any challenges that may come their way.

We've previously spoken about what makes or breaks a good relationship, including your boundaries and the things you're willing to do or not do. Having a "boundaries talk" with a new friend could be awkward, so don't do it. However, you must be honest about your limits when they arise. They won't stop until your new friend realises you don't like it when others mess with your vehicle radio.

Everything boils down to communication, or more particularly, good communication. The value of listening is often overlooked by those who pride themselves on their ability to communicate effectively. Listening is more important than speaking in good communication. Make sure you can cross off each of the **7 C's of good communication** before moving on to the next step.

Clear - What is the objective or goal of your communication? To avoid making assumptions, make your words very clear.

Concise - Try to get to the point as quickly as possible. There's no need to go around and around in circles or keep saying the same thing repeatedly.

Concrete - You have precisely the proper amount of data and facts to convey your point.

Correct - Obviously, you want to make sure you're speaking properly, but this also applies to tailoring your message to the individual. Depending on your friend's native tongue, you may need to avoid or reduce your vocabulary to communicate effectively.

Coherent - Have you ever listened to someone who switches topics quicker than you can respond? It all becomes perplexing! Maintain a rational tone in your discussion.

Courteous - We stay courteous, but it also means not being passive-aggressive or making subtle jabs at individuals.

Complete - Your message must be thorough and include all of your audience's information.

Misunderstandings in a friendship are the quickest method to tell if things aren't right. Often, a seemingly little detail is misunderstood and subsequently exaggerated. Do not hesitate to seek clarification from your buddy if you have any doubts. Make sure it doesn't destroy a nice thing by getting it straightened up.

To keep the friendship strong, here are a few additional ideas:

Agree to disagree

When you have open and honest relationships, you don't have to conceal your thoughts and feelings regarding many issues. If you and your buddy cannot agree on everything, you both should agree to disagree on certain points.

Take an active interest in them

At some point in our lives, most of us have undoubtedly found ourselves daydreaming while listening to someone else speak about something we don't care about. It's critical to actively participate in your friendships if you want to maintain a healthy dynamic. To check whether you can pique their curiosity, ask them questions. As a result, it's a two-way street where both parties benefit from each other's attention.

Try to spend quality time together as much as possible

It's up to you how much time you spend with each other and your other duties. You should choose activities that you both love and don't need your attention to be diverted by anything else. Remember that you still need time apart, so don't overdo it.

Favours and awe-inspiring surprises

Doing someone a favour is a terrific way to show your support, and doing so won't clash with your new self as long as you realise you have the power to say no when you want to. Give your buddies something unexpected as a token of your appreciation. A little gesture, such as buying them a book or tickets to a concert, might convey that you've been paying attention and that you've got their interests at heart.

Help each other out

Not just by words, but also through acts. Supporting a buddy implies that you're there to listen and give them a nice embrace or pat on the back when they need you. That also includes helping them achieve their dreams. Whether they wish to change careers or pursue a new interest, you're always there for them.

Make new memories with your friends

Make sure you don't rely on your pals for new experiences since you still need to undertake things as part of your personal development. A new activity or location to discover together might be a fun break from the routine. Consider making a bucket list of activities together and setting a deadline for when you'll fulfil them.

Making and maintaining friendships shouldn't be a chore. All of the above should come easily, or at the very least, without effort. You shouldn't try to push a friendship that isn't meant to stay; since then, it won't be real. For as long as you can maintain the channels of communication open, you will know when it is time to withdraw yourself from the friendship.

Overcoming friendship issues

There will be bumps on the road, as there are in any relationship. It's not an indication that your friendship is doomed to fail, but rather that it may need some further effort. Friendships will undergo certain modifications as a result of those in other relationships. What happens when a buddy becomes involved in a new relationship and neglects the friendships of others around them? The dynamics of a social group might also shift.

Geography may hurt a person's life. The comfort of your daily routine might be disrupted when a buddy relocates to a different city or simply a new neighbourhood. We're not as free as we'd want to be when we take on new responsibilities, or maybe new hobbies lead to a shift in our priorities.

No one is to blame for any of the issues above; it's simply a fact of life that things change, and we must evolve with them. We may get enraged, envious, or anxious when our friendships undergo a transition. Our bad feelings can't destroy our relationships at moments like these. Instead, sit down with your buddy and go through what's going on, express your thoughts, and see if you two can come up with some answers to the issues at hand.

Take some time and space if things are still raw or heated. As a result, you will be able to perceive things from a different viewpoint and put things into perspective. Use your notebook to communicate your thoughts and feelings or develop new concepts.

Refuse to accept blame placed on you by anybody other than yourself. It's pointless to assign blame until something has gone wrong since this just serves to inflame tensions. If you've done anything that's strained the relationship, own up to it and offer an apology. It may be all your buddy needs to know.

While your family and spouse may provide some of your greatest support, your friends will be there for you when you need it most. Trust, respect and clear limits are the cornerstones of every healthy relationship. Anyone shouldn't feel compelled to sacrifice their uniqueness to maintain a friendship; on the contrary, they should be encouraged to embrace their individuality.

At every level of a friendship, communication is essential. The communication expectations for the length of the friendship will be established by effective communication, which includes listening and talking, expressing one's perspective, and not concealing the truth. Since this is so important, we must get it right.

Rather than mere friendships, we'll now focus on how to be more forceful with others so that we may achieve what we want without causing offence or coming off as impolite.

Love at any cost

Many women, particularly those with the 'desire to please,' appear to have difficulty in relationships with men. These women, sometimes unwittingly, utilise their people-pleasing tendencies as invisible shackles to keep men bound to them.

A few people go to great lengths to keep their spouses from abandoning them by instilling a sense of reliance in them. As long as you do all the lovely and vital things for him, he'll never leave you alone or unhappy.

The method here utilises the people-pleaser's great fear of abandonment as a kind of manipulation. The lady works herself to exhaustion, taking care of her partner's every need to demonstrate to him just how indispensable she is. If she succeeds in getting him so reliant on her that he can't live without her, she thinks she'll be able to keep him around.

Unfortunately, putting a man into an extremely reliant position, no matter how kind and well-intended your reasons, may encourage him to do the one thing you most fear: abandon your relationship. It took Emily a long time to realise this lesson.

Emily's story

Leo and Emily had a four-year marriage. In those days, Emily did anything Leo asked of her. On their honeymoon, she declared that she would spend the rest of her life "spoiling" her spouse. For the most part, Emily focused her energies on making Leo reliant on her. Unlike her parents, to ensure that her marriage would last, she worked hard to make Leo dependent on her.

Leo had undoubtedly been spoilt after their first year together. A lack of effort on his part made him accept the fact that Emily would take care of him. Leo's sexual interest in Emily waned after the second year, notwithstanding his explanation that his lack of desire was due to "stress and job obligations." Emily never expressed dissatisfaction. Leo had a lot of sexual energy, but he didn't use it on Emily.

She determined to stay open to Leo's sexual desire if and when it resurfaced. Because she wasn't sexually pleased, she had no desire to increase his stress or make him feel horrible about himself. She believed herself to be more intelligent than that.

Emily thought she had figured out how to keep her marriage together. Leo would become completely reliant on her, to the point that he would not function without her.

It wasn't until she arrived one night to discover a note on the bed and a half-empty closet that she realised Leo had left. Because he had a new love interest, Leo claimed that he was seeking a divorce from Emily in the letter. For fear of being seen as cruel by Emily, he claimed he lacked the guts to confront her face-to-face.

'I know how much you have always done for me, and I should have been more thankful,' Leo said in a letter to me. 'Instead, I was overcome with a developing sense of resentment and even fury due to my perception of myself as a helpless and dependent person. I no longer felt like a man because I didn't believe you needed me. You're entitled to a better man. You are not to blame, Em. In my life, I've never met someone as kind as you.'

As Emily discovered, when you cultivate the seeds of imbalanced reliance in a relationship, you may reap much more than you sow. Since his excessive reliance makes him feel weak and out of control, an excessively dependent spouse is more prone to develop sentiments of resentment and hatred against his partner. In addition, he loses his self-confidence and feeling of personal independence.

It's possible that partners of people-pleasers like Leo don't even understand the severity of their anger themselves. Withholding or other passive-aggressive methods of punishment may instead be used by the spouse who is made to feel vulnerable. Leo reacted to his anger by ignoring his wife's sexual advances and by cheating on her behind her back.

You'll be pushed to reject or conceal your own needs if you're the people-pleaser in an uneven relationship like Emily. Anger and frustration are inevitable when one's emotional and sexual needs are ignored forever.

Even worse, you establish circumstances for love based on lack rather than completeness and power when you develop imbalanced reliance. As a result of this, people's self-esteem is diminished, and they are more susceptible to being exploited and feeling dissatisfied.

"I love you because I need you," is a common refrain in toxic relationships. "I need you because I love you," is a common refrain in "healthy love" partnerships. These aren't just linguistic nuances; they represent fundamentally distinct emotional states.

A healthy relationship is both mutually beneficial and mutually reinforcing. The term "balanced interdependence" refers to the fact that both partners are aware of and attentive to the demands of the other.

Memory of abuse

Many women who have been abused in the past have developed strong people-pleasing impulses as adults is both notable and alarming.

Confused sentiments about being kind and obedient arise when such distinguishing features imply that her task is to please and fulfil the sexually dominating, controlling man.

Female survivors of childhood sexual abuse sometimes describe that their abusers (often family members) would tell them to "be nice" and silently acquiesce to the demands of the sex weirdo. Both implicit and explicit threats were made that being disrespectful would result in harm.

Sexual abuse in families sometimes goes unnoticed for years until it is finally discovered. The victim is expected to safeguard the abuser and his dark secret as part of "being polite." As a result, the offender instructs the victim to treat him kindly in everyday interactions. There may be times when the abuser's actions cause the victim's behaviour to be driven by a desire to avoid more harm from the abuser.

As a result, the victim's fury has to be repressed and denied. Her fury is not focused only or even mostly on the sexually abusing parent or sibling. Often, the victim's mother or stepmother, who has failed to protect or even believe her, is the object of her rage and wrath. While the victim's people-pleasing abilities grow and are honed beneath the roof of this dysfunctional family environment, this wrath must also be controlled.

Even before she is old enough to make her own decisions, the victim's emotional wiring has already been completely twisted and knotted by the trauma she has suffered. She may blame herself for not opposing the attacker or feel terrible for being pleasant and allowing him to have his way with her.

She may have thought she wasn't lovely enough or good enough. A more rational explanation for what happened would have been if her abuser was no longer assaulting or not abusing her in the first place, she incorrectly believes. As a result, she may believe that if she had been more kind to him, he would have shown his affection more suitably, rather than sexualising and defiling the relationship.

You may find it difficult to change your people-pleasing behaviour toward men if you have been a victim of sexual abuse, but it is not impossible. Examine how your past experiences of being pleasant, compliant, and subservient to men have shaped your perceptions of sexual exploitation and abuse. However, if you think that being kind and giving men what they want or demand is a good way to defend yourself, you're right.

The core of your 'desire to please' men may be traced back to your experience of sexual abuse and your current people-pleasing tendencies. Increasing your self-awareness is the first step in making positive changes in your life.

7

Reaching your big goals and stop people-pleasing

WHEN INDIVIDUALS LOOK at their position, it might be an endless fight. People-pleasing is at the base of our self-discovery and defining what we want to accomplish to be happy. We've taken some time to do this. However, it seems as though there is still much to be done. Taking the effort to learn about yourself and build the courage to say no the proper way takes time.

In the early phases of improving my life, I realised that changing just five tiny things made a huge difference. I observed almost immediate results thanks to these five things, which were not dependent on anybody else except myself. I didn't feel like I was asking for too much since they were things I was capable of doing.

I had it in my head that modest steps would be the ones that led to the greater ones I desired. Here are the five stages we'll go through in more depth.

Step 1: Recognise unhealthy people-pleasing

People-pleasing tendencies get more and more ingrained in our character over time, to the point where they are difficult to see. It's like folks who don't realise they're continuously cursing. To put it another way, since a large number of individuals find filthy language offensive, it is simpler for others to approach them about their bad behaviour.

People-pleasing is not the same since those around you benefit from your personality. Because you are making their lives better, easier, and happier, even if they know what you are doing is wrong, they are unlikely to call attention to it.

So, it's up to you to figure out when you're trying to satisfy other people. People-pleasing traits have previously been discussed, so let's go further into how to recognise when we're about to say yes to something you don't want.

As soon as someone offers a proposal, you are overcome with emotion. It might be nervousness, sorrow, dread, fear, panic, wrath, or any other emotion. Put your finger on it, and call it what it is. You can't simply skip past the feeling.

Ask yourself what you want - this isn't a simple yes or no question. You may or may not wish to follow the advice given to you. Some portions may sound great, but you'd want to approach them differently.

The apparent response is that you need to please people, but you may need an hour at the gym or a long soak in the bathtub if you get beyond this truth.

A major portion of our desire for saying "yes" is because we are afraid of the repercussions and how the other person would respond. As a result, you may be afraid that saying yes might lead to another circumstance where you must say yes.

You are not a horrible person for saying no. In today's world, I still say yes to many things, but first, I evaluate the circumstance and determine whether I am saying yes because I feel obligated to or because I want to do so in the first place. The goal here isn't to become a jerk or someone who just looks out for themselves. We're trying to strike a delicate balance.

Becoming conscious of people-pleasing situations can help you learn what to do, even if you cannot say any right away.

Step 2: Become a grateful person

Whenever a people-pleaser gets praise, there are generally two things that follow. The shock catches us off guard, and our defensive systems, such as denial, kick in. It's difficult for us to express our gratitude in words alone.

After receiving praise, we typically strive to rationalise it. When someone compliments you on your supper, and you respond by stating it was a fortunate night or a simple recipe, you're doing yourself a favour.

Look at the following: When your spouse complements your decorating skills, you attack them because you feel like they are belittling your work. You've done more harm than good by offending them; you could even have sparked a fight. Furthermore, they will be hesitant to give you more complimentary comments in the future, which is the worst-case scenario.

I needed to retrain my brain to stop saying thank you and then continue the sentence with some kind of explanation. "Thank you" was the trigger for me to keep talking, so I decided to prevent myself from saying it. As an alternative, I've learnt these new ways of responding to a compliment:

- I respect your opinion.
- I genuinely appreciate what you did/said.
- Your warm remarks brightened my day.
- I am grateful.
- I owe you one.
- Cheers to that!

My new go-to response to the compliment "I like your haircut" is "Cheers. I appreciate that" — full stop." I would have given credit to my partner in the past, but now I'm taking the credit for my success. This behaviour is a great method for taking positive attention and not giving it away to others.

Step 3: Have self-compassion

In general, if you're dissatisfied with your life, you're also unhappy with yourself, making it difficult to love yourself. As a result, we concentrate on what we don't like about ourselves instead of focusing on what we do enjoy.

Everyday life will become more positive if you include some healthy practices to love yourself into your daily routine. Your relationship may even improve as your self-worth rises when you can accept and appreciate yourself. First, we'll look at some of the simplest techniques to cultivate self-love.

- **Keep a diary**

Writing in a diary is a great way to handle your feelings and let go of what makes you unhappy. It also helps you absorb them and focus on the positive aspects and what you've learnt from the experience later. In retrospect, it's easy to see how far you've progressed. I can't emphasise enough how important it is to maintain a diary because it allows you to express yourself without worrying about others' thoughts. Keeping a diary is an essential part of your path toward self-discovery.

- **List all of your accomplishments**

You may use this to keep your thoughts focused entirely on the good. A list of your achievements is a way to remind yourself of your abilities. It's time to enjoy your accomplishments, whether you do it with others or just by yourself. Don't be tempted to exclude anything from the list because it was someone else's idea or because you were supported by someone else.

Your accomplishments may include the following:

- Completing a project at work
- Taking a new course or finishing one
- Obtaining a personal record in a sport
- Reaching your weight loss goals

Every person's list will be unique, but no accomplishment is too small to be included.

- **Give yourself a physical and emotional break**

When we try to satisfy others, we tend to hold ourselves to their expectations and expectations of us. There is a limit to how harsh we can be on ourselves when we fall short of this ideal of perfection. Let go of the idea that you're to blame for everything that goes wrong in your life.

When it comes to coping with the stresses and strains of daily life, it's crucial to take time out for yourself physically. This is a particularly difficult task, given how much of our time is devoted to others. My recommendation is to start with five minutes a day and gradually increase it to thirty minutes as you become more comfortable. You have all of this time to yourself. If it's for you, then go ahead and meditate, stroll, read, or listen to music.

- **Have a good time alone**

At one point in my life, I hated being alone because it was a time when I could think about what might have been if I had done things differently or better. It's time to get it. If you don't like spending time with yourself, you won't be able to love yourself. If you are alone, you are not lonely. It allows you to try new things and learn what you like and don't like about them on your own, without the pressure of being around other people.

- **Release yourself from your mistake agreement**

Everyone takes a trip down memory lane and reflects on their errors simply because no human being has ever made a mistake in their lives. It's a good idea to look at these blunders as a way to discover more about yourself. However, you must forgive and move on from your mistakes if you want to love yourself.

Travelling is a once-in-a-lifetime opportunity, and the first time you do it, you'll want to do it again. It's possible to learn about oneself in a new way when travelling alone since you're exposed to various environments and civilisations. When you're alone, you can be who you are without worrying about what other people think or feel.

You should and may begin the process of learning to appreciate and appreciate yourself right now. It's all in your head and heart. You don't have to be afraid of anybody else's viewpoint, and you don't have to worry about offending anyone. Nobody will even notice that you're doing these things.

When I realised that I was able to make little improvements right quickly, it gave me an incredible sense of accomplishment. Because I didn't have to tell anybody about it, I was able to discover more about myself because I didn't have to worry about the repercussions. The majority of self-acceptance advice will become a natural part of your life. Others may be less frequent, but even now, fifteen years later, I still maintain a journal in which I keep track of my accomplishments. I also go on a vacation once a year, whether it's for a few days or a few weeks. As a nice way of saying, "No, not this time," I smile when people ask if they may join me.

Step 4: Prioritise your goals

We live in a society where it is considered selfish or uncharitable to put one's interests ahead of others. While some individuals seem to have a natural talent for this, others have to learn. People-pleasing makes it almost impossible, and although the principle is straightforward, putting it into action may be difficult. Before we go into prioritising your demands, let's take a look at why it's necessary.

You face the danger of exhaustion and fatigue if you can't put your own needs ahead of others. If everyone expects you to help them, you'll become overextended and unable to assist anybody. It makes me think of how important it is to put on your oxygen mask before helping others while flying. You deserve to take care of your own needs and be content, but if you're a people-pleaser, you could overlook this point.

"Learn to say no" was one of the first things I came across when I started looking for a solution to my problem, but I needed something I could practice right away. Here's how to prioritise your own needs without resorting to the no word right away.

Say yes to yourself

This is a personal favourite of mine. For the first time in a long time, I was able to say "no" instead of "yes." To say yes to others, we must be able to say no to ourselves. In the future, no matter how few, say yes to your demands.

Find strategies to save time

Whether it's a game on your phone or a post on social media, we all have habits that take up valuable time throughout the day. You'll have more time for yourself if you can get rid of those items.

Write down what you need to do, and don't include anything that other people need of you. If you have a specific goal in mind, put it in your list of things to do (not have to do).

The time you saved may be put to good use, so don't waste it on non-essential tasks like checking on your friends or running an errand for your coworkers. It's time for you to enjoy the time you've freed up for yourself.

Developing a routine will offer you a higher chance of reaching your requirements in the early stages since they are already part of your routine. At other times, we will wish to break out of the pattern.

Adjust your mentality

This one is a little trickier, but it doesn't need saying any to anybody. Take a few quiet deep breaths and tell yourself that you deserve to put your needs first when you feel guilty.

Once you begin to grant yourself some time each day, it becomes simpler to envisage spending an entire day with yourself. Things you need to do and things you want to do should be mixed on this day.

Step 5. Create a mantra for yourself

It is common to use a mantra to incite the desired behaviour change. However, we want to use them to change some of our behaviours rather than only for emotional or physical reasons.

A short period is all it takes for the effects of a mantra or affirmation to become apparent. The positive ideas and energy you give to your mind by repeating your mantra will lead to the alterations in your mind that you need and want. When it comes to mantras, you may either look for inspiration online or come up with one of your own.

People-pleasing results from a mental and emotional desire to please people to the fullest degree possible, regardless of the consequences. It's easy for us to forget about our own needs and emotions. It is the goal of a mantra to remove shame and the belief that you are less than others.

Using the following mantras, a people-pleaser attitude may be conquered:

- You're really valuable. It's important to consider what I want.
- I deserve to be happy. I am strong.
- I'm feeling good about myself.
- My goals are important. I'm still a good person.
- I'm proud of myself.

You'll notice that none of these brief phrases includes any negative language or discusses the future. Your conscious and subconscious mind will be reminded of the changes you want due to using these tools.

If you're having trouble sleeping, use mantras and affirmations to help you wind down for the night and get a good night's rest.

Going on a trip by yourself right now is too much for you. Telling people and explaining why you're doing so may make you feel compelled to do so. People-pleasing is a problem that you may not want to confront with others, particularly if your loved ones are worried and try to talk you out of taking a break from your life. For this reason, we start small when it comes to making changes that will have an influence on our lives and help us go to the next level.

. . .

ALL OF THE ideas we've explored are fantastic ways to keep progressing toward saying no and achieving your goal. You'll be more equipped to set boundaries in your relationships and other aspects of your life after you've experienced the advantages of these tips. Next, we'll look at why and how boundaries are established. One of the biggest fears we have is being rejected, and we're going to discover how to overcome this fear.

8

Set healthy boundaries without fear

EVERYONE NEEDS BOUNDARIES, but people-pleasers need them much more. Life would be a sea of drab if we had no limits to keep us in check. We value being able to gratify people and will do so as long as the grey continues. As the line between black and white, a boundary informs us of our limits regarding mental and emotional pressure. Boundaries are a means for people-pleasers to take care of themselves while also showing others what they can and cannot do and what they should and should not do for them.

With no boundaries, a people-pleaser will keep making reasons to get what they want to satisfy others. When we don't have clear boundaries in place, it's much simpler to put the needs of others ahead of our own. As we give up our identities to get the love we need, we gradually lose whatever limits we had, assuming they ever were in the first place.

Defining a boundary

A boundary is a line or partition that separates two or more areas. Whether it's a physical or emotional barrier, separators may be used to separate you from others. You must decide for yourself what is and isn't appropriate in a given setting. People will know how to treat you if you set a boundary.

In many cases, touch is linked to physical limits. Huggers and non-huggers may be found all over the globe. The hugger will cross the non-hugger line and embrace them when the two meet. The hugger doesn't see anything wrong with this, while the non-hugger finds it very distressing.

The restrictions we impose on our emotions are known as emotional boundaries. An example of this would be a joking or sarcastic comment. Jokes might start as innocent fun, but the victim suffers an emotional or physical reaction as soon as they cross the line.

It wouldn't have been an issue if the hugger and the joker were mindful of the other people's limits. We aren't attempting to lay blame, as we did when examining the origins of people-pleasing. Everyone is accountable for their actions (such as the hug or the joke), but it is also important that we know our limits and do not hesitate to express them to others around us when necessary.

Examples of healthy and unhealthy boundaries

The capacity to say no as a good habit is intentionally omitted since it is self-evident. In the last several months, progress has been made in overcoming our unhealthy boundaries. Rather, consider some more examples of good and bad boundaries.

Healthy boundaries

- Personal values and ideas should not be sacrificed for the sake of others.
- Being able to express one's feelings freely.
- Acknowledging and celebrating your value.
- Showing consideration for the thoughts, emotions, and opinions of others.
- Recognising social signals before going out of limits.

Unhealthy Boundaries

- Giving up your beliefs to fit in with the group.
- Trying to hide your feelings or blaming yourself for the feelings of others.
- Not prioritising your self-worth in favour of others'.
- Disrespecting or demeaning the views of those with whom you disagree.
- Inappropriate contact, whether sexual or otherwise.

You may think of your relationships as a scale with your values and views on one side and another person's values and ideas. There must be a set of limits that each person is aware of and respects for the relationship to remain balanced.

People-pleasers have difficulty establishing healthy boundaries because they don't value their own emotions and goals in life sufficiently. Not necessarily because they aim to abuse the relationship, but because they don't know their limits, people-pleasers find themselves in the company of narcissists. We can't expect people to know our limits if we don't properly establish them.

Understanding what constitutes appropriate conduct in a relationship is the first step in ensuring that people respect your boundaries. By setting limits, individuals who care about you will better understand your needs and capabilities, which should lessen the need for you to say no. Having less to do for people and not worrying about disrupting the dynamics of a relationship is a wonderful feeling.

Let's have a look at some measures to follow so that we may work on setting varied healthy boundaries within our relationships because each sort of connection will demand a distinct set of limits.

Setting healthy boundaries in your relationships with friends

Arguably, the most important components of a strong friendship are trust and open communication. Friendships may be formed at an early age, and some of these friendships last a lifetime. Anyone who genuinely cares about you will appreciate and even support your choice to establish limits in your friendship if they truly love you for who you are. This is because they care about your well-being.

At the same time, it's possible that establishing limits in a connection may help you identify your true friends. Boundaries that are disrespected already constitute boundary violations. You are the only one who can determine who you want to spend time with. In the end, my recommendation is to use these activities to examine the roots of your friendships and begin cutting links with those who aren't ready to accept your new, healthy boundaries.

Take a trip down memory lane and retrace the course of your relationship. Is there a repeating theme in your connection with your buddy in which they have offended you or made you feel uncomfortable? If this is the case, you may enhance your connection by establishing limits based on previous incidents.

Listen to what your body has to say. When a difficult scenario arises between you and a buddy, it's normal to feel queasy in the stomach. At this point, you need to take a step back and figure out what's wrong with your relationship with this buddy.

Think about what you're going to say to your buddy before you do it. We'll naturally avoid having this talk because we're afraid of the repercussions. Remind yourself that you're not doing anything wrong, and this will keep you going. Not that you don't care about your friends and family, but only that you need to put more effort into your well-being. Remind yourself that this isn't selfish and that you're trying to enhance your connection with the person you're talking to.

Talk to your friend about your new boundaries at the right moment. When they've gone too far, arrived too late, or continued to speak about their issues for too long, that's the best moment to confront them. It will be simpler for your buddy to understand and appreciate the new boundaries that you have established.

Choosing the right words is essential. The use of harsh phrases like "I detest it when...," which might ellicit unpleasant feelings such as anger, should be avoided. As an alternative, begin your sentence with the words "It would make me feel more at ease if...".

Talk to a buddy about your anxieties about communicating your feelings. Most of your time will be spent listening to their concerns if you're a people-pleaser. If this is the case, they may be unfamiliar with you expressing your feelings rather than fearing their reply. A simple chat about your anxieties with a real friend can balance out the "therapy sessions," allowing you to speak about your feelings.

If your friends do anything that bothers you, politely point it out to them. People who are consistently late for appointments bother me since it suggests that they don't appreciate my time. However, I never felt comfortable telling anybody about it. It was helpful for me to start by telling a buddy in a lighthearted manner with a smile. "You know it drives me insane when you're late," for example. I had no business becoming angry in the first place. The next time we established a plan, my follow-up question was, "You're not going to be late, are you?". Fortunately, the issue was resolved, and I understood that even though we may fear the worst when it comes to our friends, people who care about us don't want to harm us.

As the last step, start with a trusted friend who will be more understanding and appreciative of the limits you intend to establish. Friends who may require a stronger hand in respecting your limits will gain trust in your determination due to this.

Family relationships: How to set healthy boundaries

Our connections with our families might be more complicated than those we have with other people. There may have been moments of stress, broken families, deaths, money problems, or simply conflicts of personalities in the past that have not been handled. It is more difficult to break apart from dysfunctional familial ties. To avoid upsetting others, people-pleasers become more subservient and allow others to behave and say as they see fit.

In familial settings, you will know what causes you to feel uneasy or even sick in the pit of your stomach. Therefore you need to be mindful of these feelings. The annoying aunt who always makes comparisons between you and your relatives or the competitive sibling might be blamed. Make a mental note of your triggers, no matter what they are, to determine what boundaries you need to establish.

In the same way, you should never feel guilty about prioritising your interests above your family's. You should keep this in mind as you get ready to conduct the conversation about boundaries.

I began practising coping methods, for this reason, a few weeks before talking to my family. I would use my coping strategy if I felt that one of my boundaries had been crossed. Doodling on a sheet of paper on my balcony, ideally when the cold night air soothed my overheated body, was how I did this.

As you prepare to talk about boundaries with your family, you may want to try some of these coping mechanisms:

- Using a cushion to scream/yell.
- Dancing to your favourite songs while listening to them.
- Taking a hot shower or bath is an excellent way to relax.
- Working out.
- Mindfulness, meditation, and yoga.
- Getting a massage or pampering yourself.

Keep in mind that certain members of your family may be so worried about you that the concept that you need limits might hurt them and make them feel guilty for what they have put you through. They may.

If you're going to create boundaries with your family members, you need to be mindful of what might happen. Doing so is not an excuse. I used this as a coping method to help my mother come to terms with the reality that I wasn't content with my life. From then on, all I had to do was smile and say, "Mum, remember our little discussion," whenever our new imaginary boundary seemed to be ready to be crossed, and bless her, she would always react with a, "Yes, yes, you are right, darling."

Family members that don't respect your boundaries won't be easy to get away from. With practice and the techniques in this book, you will be able to say no to circumstances that lead to your family members overstepping your boundaries in the future.

Workplace boundaries: How to set them right

Relationships at work might be much more difficult to navigate than those with friends and members of our families. We have no option but to spend an average of eight hours a day with our co-workers regarding our professions. When working from home, you still have to maintain constant contact with your co-workers.

Aside from these factors, employees are likely to come and often go due to low employee retention, making it difficult to cultivate close working connections with co-workers and create the confidence to assert your preferences and needs.

It is simpler for individuals who aren't prone to pleasing others to point out breaches of the rules as soon as they happen. The constant turnover of workers might make it even more difficult for a people-pleaser to set limits.

Even if you've only worked with someone for a few weeks, months, or even years, the roots of your professional connection and friendship are likely already in place. My advice would be to follow the stages in building boundaries with friends, but combine this with coping mechanisms that we did with our families, even if you may have to adapt some for the workplace environment.

This combo works effectively because we need to learn to deal with these feelings as soon as they arise so that they don't increase. To calm down after a heated argument, you may walk away from the person you're upset with. However, you will almost certainly face the repercussions of your absence from work.

For new co-workers, this is the most frightening. You may put your newfound knowledge to use right immediately, without fear of harming individuals you care about:

Whenever the subject of values is brought up, be sure to let others know about them. You should never compromise your core principles, especially today when they might reveal a lot about your work ethic.

If you are confident, you may begin to express your thoughts as soon as possible. As an alternative, express your thoughts in the context of a team, such as "Perhaps it would be better if we considered..."

Get everyone on the same page about your timetable from the start. They are less likely to transgress your limits if they are aware of them, such as that you are unavailable at particular times of the day.

Do not use "fluff" to justify your explanations. In the job, emotional reasons are typical of little help to people-pleasers. Telling someone, you're unable to perform anything just serves to focus attention on your shortcomings. "If I do [X], I won't be able to do [Y], and the customer is counting on this," or "If I do [Y], the client is counting on [Y], and this is the only way I can accomplish [Y]."

Conclusion

Now that you've finished this book, I hope you're ready to go on new self-acceptance and interpersonal harmony path. You've gone from being a people-pleaser to being more in charge of your own life and more conscious of your ability to change.

Now that you've learned how to identify a problem in your life and formulate a plan to repair or enhance it, it's time to put your plan into action. If you've overcome your longstanding 'desire to please,' it's possible to retake control over practically any element of your behaviour, looks, health habits, relationships, ideas, or emotions.

It is powerful to go through personal growth firsthand rather than merely learn about it. The dedication, discipline, and fortitude required to conquer your 'desire to please' are commendable. Your newly reclaimed standing should be guarded against those who would rather see you return to your old people-pleasing ways.

Make a point of putting your newfound self-care goals into action and being cautious about how you react to the needs of others. Replace the obsessive people-pleasing behaviour with positive choices based on caring for yourself and others.

Feedback

Thank you for reading 'How To Stop Giving Yourself Away.' I sincerely hope you enjoyed and got value from this book, and that it helps you to forge those all-important positive habits that will bring peace and harmony to your life from this moment on.

If you have a free moment, please leave me some feedback on Amazon.

Also, scan the QR code below to visit the Hackney and jones Publishing website where you can find more information on the range of books available.

 HackneyandJones.com

www.ingramcontent.com/pod-product-compliance
Lightning Source LLC
Chambersburg PA
CBHW031546080526
44588CB00018B/2714